AF540318

ECO-TOURISM

By

Jack Randall

DISCOVERY PUBLISHING HOUSE PVT. LTD.
NEW DELHI-110 002

Published by:
Tilak Wasan

DISCOVERY PUBLISHING HOUSE PVT. LTD.
4831/24, Ansari Road, Prahlad Street
Darya Ganj, New Delhi-110002 (India)
Phone: +91-11-23279245, 43764432
Fax: +91-11-23253475
E-mail: parul.wasan@gmail.com
discoverypublishinghouse@gmail.com
info@discoverypublishinggroup.com
web: www.discoverypublishinggroup.com

***First Edition:* 2011**
ISBN: 978-81-8356-887-6

Eco-tourism

Reprinted - 2017

Printed at:
Infinity Imaging Systems
Delhi

PREFACE

If Ecotourism is to be viewed as a tool for rural development, it must also help shift economic and political control to the local community, village, cooperative, or entrepreneur. This is the most difficult and time-consuming principle in the economic equation and the one that foreign opeators and "partners" most often let fall through the cracks or that they follow only partially or formally.

Responsible ecotourism includes programs that minimize the negative aspects of conventional tourism on the environment and enhance the cultural integrity of local people. Therefore, in addition to evaluating environmental and cultural factors, an integral part of ecotourism is the promotion of recycling, energy efficiency, water conservation, and creation of economic opportunities for local communities.

Ecotourism is a form of tourism that involves traveling to tranquil and unpolluted natural areas. According to the definition and principles of ecotourism established by The International Ecotourism Society (TIES) in 1990, ecotourism is Responsible travel to natural areas that conserves the environment and improves the well-being of local people.

Ecotourism, responsible tourism, jungle tourism, and sustainable development have become prevalent concepts since the late 1980s, and ecotourism has experienced arguably the fastest growth of all sub-sectors in the tourism industry. The popularity represents a change in tourist perceptions, increased environmental awareness, and a desire to explore natural environments. At times, such changes become as much a statement affirming one's social identity, educational sophistication, and disposable income as it has about preserving the Amazon rainforest or the Caribbean reef for posterity.

CONTENTS

Chapter-1

CONCEPT OF ECO-TOURISM

Defining "Ecotourism" a has proven to be a difficult task given all the different players attempting to define it. People tend to define things in terms that are beneficial to themselves, hence the variety of definitions. There are however several workable definitions currently in wide use.

"Ecotourism is ecologically sustainable tourism with a primary focus on experiencing natural areas that fosters environmental and cultural understanding, appreciation and conservation".

The EcoGuide Australia program provides a credential, endorsing the recipient as a guide who will deliver an authentic, environmentally responsible, and professional ecotourism experience. The EcoGuide Program also provides guides with a cost effective and convenient advantage in being able to attain both EcoGuide and the national Guides of Australia (GOA) accreditation in one application.

The EcoGuide Australia Certification Program was originally developed out of a pilot program driven by Australia's guides and the tourism industry. Ecotourism Australia manages the EcoGuide Program, backed by the expertise of its management team. We also maintain a team of independent assessors who will examine your EcoGuide application.

The International Ecotourism Society defines Ecotourism as: "responsible travel to natural areas that conserves the environment and improves the welfare of local people".

The Australian Commission on National Ecotourism Strategy calls it: "nature-based tourism that involves education and interpretation of the natural environment and is managed to be ecologically sustainable".

Since the publication of her excellent book "Ecotourism and Sustainable Development" Martha Honey's definition is quickly becoming the standard. Most serious studies of ecotourism including several University programs now use this as the working definition. Here then are her 7 defining points:

1. Involves travel to natural destinations. These destinations are often remote areas, whether inhabited or uninhabited, and are usually under some kind of environmental protection at the national, international, communal or private level.

2. Minimizes Impact. Tourism causes damage. Ecotourism strives to minimize the adverse affects of hotels, trails, and other infrastructure by using either recycled materials or plentyfully available local building materials, renewable sources of energy, recycling and safe disposal of waste and garbage, and environmentally and culturally sensitive architectural design. Minimization of impact also requires that the numbers and mode of behavior of tourists be regulated to ensure limited damage to the ecosystem.

3. Builds environmental awareness. Ecotourism means education, for both tourists and residents of nearby communities. Well before departure tour operators should supply travelers with reading material about the country, environment and local people, as well as a code of conduct for both the traveler and the industry itself. This information helps prepare the tourist as The Ecotourism Societies guidelines state"to learn about the places and peoples visited" and "to minimize their negative impacts while visiting sensitive environments and cultures".

Essential to good ecotourism are well-trained, multilingual naturalist guides with skills in natural and cultural history, environmental interpretation, ethical principles and effective communication. Ecotourism projects should also help educate members of the surrounding community, schoolchildren and the broader public in the host country. To do so they must offer greatly reduced entrance and lodge fees for nationals and free educational trips for local students and those living near thetourist attraction.

4. Provides direct financial benefits for consevation: Ecotourism helps raise funds for environmental protection, research and education through a variety of mechanisms, including park entrance fees, tour company, hotel, airline and airport taxes and voluntary contributions.

5. Provides financial benefits and empowerment for local people: National Parks and other conservation areas will only survive if there are "happy people" around their perimeters. The local community must be involved with and receive income and other tangible benefits(potable water, roads, health clinics, etc.) from the conservation area and it's tourist facilities. Campsites, lodges, guide services, restaurants and other concessions should be run by or in partnership with communities surrounding a park or other tourist destination. More importantly, if Ecotourism is to be viewed as a tool for rural development, it must also help shift economic and political control to the local community, village, cooperative, or entrepreneur. This is the most difficult and time-consuming principle in the economic equation and the one that foreign opeators and "partners" most often let fall through the cracks or that they follow only partially or formally.

6. Respects local culture: Ecotourism is not only "greener" but also less culturally intrusive and exploitative than conventional tourism. Whereas prostitution, black markets and drugs often are by-products of mass tourism, ecotourism stives to be culturally respectful and have a

minimal effect on both the natural environment and the human population of a host country. This is not easy, especially since ecotourism often involves travel to remote areas where small and isolate communities have had little experience interacting with foreigners. And like conventional tourism, ecotourism involves an unequal relationship of power between the visitor and the host and a commodification of the relationship through exchange of money. Part of being a responsible ecotourist is learning beforehand about the local customs, respecting dress codes and other social norms and not intruding on the community unless either invited or as part of a well organized tour.

7. Supports human rights and democratic movements: Although tourism often is glibly hailed as a tool for building international understanding and world peace, this does not happen automatically; frequently in fact tourism bolsters the economies of repressive and undemocratic states. Mass tourism pays scant attention to the political system of the host country or struggles within it, unless civil unrest spills over into attacks on tourists. Ecotourism demands a more holistic approach to travel, one in which participants strive to respect, learn about and benefit both the local environment and local communities. Although not part of The Ecotourism Societies definition, giving economic benefits and showing cultural sensitivities to local communities cannot be seperated from understanding their political circumstances. In many developing countries, rural populations living around national parks and other ecotourism attractions are locked in contests with the national government and multinational corporations for control of the assets and their benfits. Ecotourist therefore need to be sensitive to the host country's political environment and social climate and need to consider the merits of international boycotts called for by those supporting democratic reforms,

majority rule, and human rights. For example the campaign by the African National Congress(ANC) to isolate South Africa through a boycott of investment, trade, sports and tourism helped bring down apartheid. Determining whether to boycott or visit a country is not always easy. Among the questions to ask are: Does the economic growth fueled by tourism really improve the chances of human rights being respected? Will boycotting a country harm already impoverished workers more than it will corporate or government titans? Or are the short term economic penalties more than offset by the ultimate benefits of change? If one visits a repressive state like China, Indonesia, Peru or Syria, it is possible to make the trip rewarding both personally and politically by consciously learning about the country beforehand, meeting with dissidents and average folks, as well as government officials while there, and speaking about the political climate, not just the weather after returning home.

About Ecotourism Australia

Ecotourism Australia was formed in 1991 as an incorporated NPO, and is the peak national body for the ecotourism industry.

Get to know your Ecotourism Australia Board

Ecotourism Australia is steered by a highly experienced team drawn from diverse areas within the tourism industry.

Eco Certification Program

The Eco Certification Program is a world first. It has been developed by industry for industry, addressing the need to identify genuine ecotourism and nature tourism operators in Australia.

Ecoguide Australia Program

The new 2007 EcoGuide Australia Certification Program is an industry driven certification program for nature and ecotour guides. It provides an industry credential that rewards guides that achieve and maintain specified competencies and standards. EcoGuide now also includes the new national Guides of Australia accreditation at no extra cost.

The Ecotourism Australia Vision

"To be leaders in assisting ecotourism and other committed tourism operations to become environmentally sustainable, economically viable, and socially and culturally responsible".

Ecotourism Australia Mission Statement

Ecotourism Australia's Mission is about growing, consolidating and promoting ecotourism and other committed tourism operations to become more sustainable, through approaches such as:

- developing and adopting standards for sustainable practices
- increasing the professionalism of those working within the tourism industry
- streamlining policies and processes that have in the past complicated operating in protected areas
- assisting operators to improve the quality of interpretation offered about the places they visit
- improving positioning and financial viability for operators who adopt sustainable practices
- contributing to conservation solutions and projects; involving and providing benefits to local communities
- marketing the principles of sustainability to increase awareness across the tourism industry

The Nature and Ecotourism Accreditation Program

The Eco Certification Program is Ecotourism Australia's flagship program. Ecotourism and nature tourism accreditation provide industry, protected area managers, local communities and travellers with an assurance that an accredited product is backed by a commitment to best practice ecological sustainability, natural area management and the provision of quality ecotourism experiences. Developed in Australia, the Eco Certification Program is now being exported to the rest of the world as the International Ecctourism Standard. Successful completion of Eco Certification Program includes Membership of Ecotourism Australia.

The EcoGuide Certification Program

The EcoGuide Australia Certification Program is an industry driven certification program for nature and ecotour guides. It provides an industry credential that rewards guides that achieve specified competencies and standards. The program is designed to enhance Guides competencies, and assess a Guides skills, knowledge, personal attributes and actions. The EcoGuide Australia Certification Program compliments and supports the Eco Certification Program. Successful achievement of EcoGuide Certification includes Membership of Ecotourism Australia and attractive professional development and networking opportunities.

Other Association activities

In addition to the operation of the Eco Certification Program and the EcoGuide Australia program, Ecotourism Australia is active in a range of areas including:

- an on-line searchable database of EA members available through our website
- a monthly electronic newsletter and email group for members

- lobbying for decisions and initiatives that improve the viability of the ecotourism industry
- advocating for sustainable practices to be implemented across the tourism industry
- seminars and workshops on marketing, ecotourism business management, sustainable practices, the Eco Certification Program, Eco-guiding issues and training
- production of a range of publications
- a lively, interesting and informative annual national conference held in a region with local ecotourism options

Eco-tourism is more than a catch phrase for nature loving travel and recreation. Eco-tourism is consecrated for preserving and sustaining the diversity of the world's natural and cultural environments. It accommodates and entertains visitors in a way that is minimally intrusive or destructive to the environment and sustains & supports the native cultures in the locations it is operating in. Responsibility of both travellers and service providers is the genuine meaning for eco-tourism.

Eco-tourism also endeavours to encourage and support the diversity of local economies for which the tourism-related income is important. With support from tourists, local services and producers can compete with larger, foreign companies and local families can support themselves. Besides all these, the revenue produced from tourism helps and encourages governments to fund conservation projects and training programs.

Saving the environment around you and preserving the natural luxuries and forest life, that's what eco-tourism is all about. Whether it's about a nature camp or organizing trekking trips towards the unspoilt and inaccessible regions, one should always keep in mind not to create any mishap or disturbance in the life cycle of nature.

Eco-tourism focuses on local cultures, wilderness adventures, volunteering, personal growth and learning new ways to live on our vulnerable planet. It is typically defined as travel to destinations where the flora, fauna, and cultural heritage are the primary attractions. Responsible Eco-tourism includes programs that minimize the adverse effects of traditional tourism on the natural environment, and enhance the cultural integrity of local people. Therefore, in addition to evaluating environmental and cultural factors, initiatives by hospitality providers to promote recycling, energy efficiency, water reuse, and the creation of economic opportunities for local communities are an integral part of Eco-tourism.

Historical, biological and cultural conservation, preservation, sustainable development etc. are some of the fields closely related to Eco-Tourism. Many professionals have been involved in formulating and developing eco-tourism policies. They come from the fields of Geographic Information Systems, Wildlife Management, Wildlife Photography, Marine Biology and Oceanography, National and State Park Management, Environmental Sciences, Women in Development, Historians and Archaeologists, etc.

Eco-tourism is considered the fastest growing market in the tourism industry, according to the World Tourism Organization with an annual growth rate of 5% worldwide and representing 6% of the world gross domestic product, 11.4% of all consumer spending - not a market to be taken lightly.

What is Eco-tourism?

Fundamentally, eco-tourism means making as little environmental impact as possible and helping to sustain the indigenous populace, thereby encouraging the preservation of wildlife and habitats when visiting a place. This is responsible form of tourism and tourism development, which encourages going back to natural products in every aspect of life. It is also the key to sustainable ecological development.

The International Eco-tourism Society defines eco-tourism as "responsible travel to natural areas that conserves the environment and improves the well-being of local people." This means that those who implement and participate in Eco-tourism activities should follow the following principles:

- Minimize impact
- Build environmental and cultural awareness and respect
- Provide positive experiences for both visitors and hosts
- Provide direct financial benefits for conservation
- Provide financial benefits and empowerment for local people
- Raise sensitivity to host countries' political, environmental, and social climate
- Support international human rights and labour agreements

Aware of the Environment - Today the "Green Laws" of conservation are making people aware of how man and the environment can live symbiotically for more time to come and eco-tourism is the only way to maximize the economic, environmental and social benefits of tourism. Everyone is a stakeholder in the process and we clearly need to avoid our past shortcomings and negative impact that they have had.

In India too the movement is gathering momentum with more and more travel and travel related organisation's are addressing the needs of the eco-tourists and promoting eco-tourism in the country. Some basic do's and don'ts of eco-tourism are listed below:

Do's

Carry back all non-degradable litter such as empty bottles, tins, plastic bags etc. These must not litter the environment or be buried. They must be disposed in municipal dustbins only. Observe the sanctity of holy sites, temples and local cultures.

Cut noise pollution. Do not blare aloud radios, tape recorders or other electronic entertainment equipment in nature resorts, sanctuaries and wildlife parks.

In case temporary toilets are set-up near campsites, after defecation, cover with mud or sand. Make sure that the spot is at least 30 meters away from the water source. Respect people's privacy while taking photographs. Ask for prior permission before taking a photograph.

Don'ts

Do not take away flora and fauna in the forms of cuttings, seeds or roots. It is illegal, especially in the Himalayas. The environment is really delicate in this region and the bio-diversity of the region has to be protected at all costs.

Do not use pollutants such as detergent, in streams or springs while washing and bathing.

Do not use wood as fuel to cook food at the campsite.

Do not leave cigarettes butts or make open fires in the forests.

Do not consume aerated drinks, alcohol, drugs or any other intoxicant and throw bottles in the wild.

Do not tempt the locals, especially children by offering them foodstuff or sweets. Respect local traditions.

Polythene and plastics are non biodegradable and unhealthy for the environment and must not be used and littered.

As a traveller, you will have an impact on the environment and culture of the place you are visiting. Here are some rules of thumb to make this impact positive!

Golden Rules When You Travel

Learn about your destination before you get there. Read guidebooks, travel articles, histories, and/or novels by local authors and pay particular attention to customs such as greetings, appropriate dress, eating behaviours, etc. Being sensitive to these customs will increase local acceptance of you as a tourist and enrich your trip.

Follow established guidelines. Ask your eco-tour operator, guide and/or the local authorities what their guidelines are for limiting tourism's impact on the environment and local culture. Staying on trails, packing up your trash, and remaining set distances away from wildlife are a few ways to minimize your impact in sensitive areas.

Seek out and support locally owned businesses. Support local businesses during your eco-travels to ensure maximum community and conservation benefit from your spending.

Eco-Tourism in India is still at a very nascent stage, but there are for sure conscious efforts to save the fragile Himalayan Eco System and culture and heritage of the indigenous people, which is probably the largest concentration in the world.

Holiday Camping vis a vis Hotel accommodation are gathering momentum amongst the metropolis traveller. A plethora of holiday camping options are available in the Himalayan belt, where soft adventure tourism is packaged with holiday camping to create an acceptable eco-tourism product. Resorts tucked deep inside jungles of Karnataka, House-boats of Kerala, Tree Houses at Vythiri combine to make India one of the most diverse eco-tourism destinations on the planet. Some of these are given below

Eco-Tourism Pioneers in Kerala - http://www.tourindiakerala.com Jungle Lodges and Resorts - (Eco-Tourism Pioneers in South India) - http://www.junglelodges.com

The Camp RapidFire - Rishikesh, Uttaranchal

The Camp BodhiSatva - Rajgarh, Himachal Pradesh

The Himalayan Trout House - Tirthan, Himachal Pradesh - www.questrails.com

Info on Organic Farming & Eco-Tourism:

The Saat-tal Camp - Saat-tal, Nainital

The Camp Purple - Mukteshwar

The Camp Kyari (one of the finest models of Eco-tourism in the country) - Village Kyari, Ramnagar - www.wildrift.com

Camp Silver Sands - Rishikesh, Uttaranchal

Camp Lunagarh - Mori, Uttaranchal - www.treknraft.com

The Himalayan River Runner Camp - Rishikesh, Uttaranchal - www.hrr.com

The OAI Camp - Rishikesh, Uttaranchal - www.oai.com

The Leopard Beach Camp - Rishikesh, Uttaranchal - www.snowleopardadventures.com

Responsible ecotourism includes programs that minimize the negative aspects of conventional tourism on the environment and enhance the cultural integrity of local people. Therefore, in addition to evaluating environmental and cultural factors, an integral part of ecotourism is the promotion of recycling, energy efficiency, water conservation, and creation of economic opportunities for local communities.

Ecotourism is a form of tourism that involves traveling to tranquil and unpolluted natural areas. According to the definition and principles of ecotourism established by The International Ecotourism Society (TIES) in 1990, ecotourism is "Responsible travel to natural areas that conserves the environment and improves the well-being of local people." (TIES, 1990). Martha Honey, expands on the TIES definition by describing the seven characteristics of ecotourism, which are:

- Involves travel to natural destinations.
- Minimizes impact and
- Builds environmental awareness.
- Provides direct financial benefits for conservation.

- Provides financial benefits and empowerment for local people.
- Respects local culture.
- Supports human rights and democratic movements.

Ideally, ecotourism should satisfy several criteria, such as:

- conservation of biological diversity and cultural diversity through ecosystem protection
- promotion of sustainable use of biodiversity, by providing jobs to local populations
- sharing of socio-economic benefits with local communities and indigenous peoples by having their informed consent and participation in the management of ecotourism enterprises
- tourism to unspoiled natural resources, with minimal impact on the environment being a primary concern.
- minimization of tourism's own environmental impact
- affordability and lack of waste in the form of luxury
- local culture, flora and fauna being the main attractions

For many countries, ecotourism is not simply a marginal activity to finance protection of the environment, but is a major industry of the national economy. For example, in Costa Rica, Ecuador, Nepal, Kenya, Madagascar and Antarctica, ecotourism represents a significant portion of the gross domestic product and economic activity.

The concept of ecotourism is widely misunderstood and in practice is often used as a marketing tool to promote tourism that is related to nature. This is an especially frequent malpractice in the realm of Jungle tourism. Critics claim that these greenwashing practices, carried out in the name of ecotourism, often consist of placing a hotel in a splendid landscape, to the detriment of the ecosystem. According to them, ecotourism must above all sensitize people to the beauty and the fragility of nature. They condemn some operators as greenwashing their operations: using the labels of "green" and "eco-friendly", while behaving in environmentally irresponsible ways.

Although academics disagree about who can be classified as an ecotourist and there is little statistical data, some estimate that more than five million ecotourists - the majority of the ecotourist population - come from the United States, with many others from Western Europe, Canada and Australia.

Currently, there are various moves to create national and international ecotourism accreditation programs, although the process is also controversial. National ecotourism certification programs have been put in place in countries such as Costa Rica, Australia, Kenya and Sweden.

History

Hector Ceballos-Lascurain coined the term 'ecotourism' in July 1983, when he was performing the dual role of Director General of Standards and Technology of SEDUE (the Mexican Ministry of Urban Development and Ecology) and founding president of PRONATURA (an influential Mexican conservationist NGO). PRONATURA was lobbying for the conservation of the wetlands in northern Yucatan as breeding and feeding habitats of the American Flamingo. Source: Conversation

Ecotourism, responsible tourism, jungle tourism, and sustainable development have become prevalent concepts since the late 1980s, and ecotourism has experienced arguably the fastest growth of all sub-sectors in the tourism industry. The popularity represents a change in tourist perceptions, increased environmental awareness, and a desire to explore natural environments. At times, such changes become as much a statement affirming one's social identity, educational sophistication, and disposable income as it has about preserving the Amazon rainforest or the Caribbean reef for posterity.

Definitional Problems and Greenwashing

Part of the problem, a clear definition must delineate what is, and is not, ecotourism. Ideally, ecotourism satisfies several general criteria, including the conservation of biological diversity and cultural diversity through ecosystem protection, promotion of sustainable use of biodiversity, share of social-economic benefits with local communities through informed consent and participation, increase in environmental and cultural knowledge, affordability and reduced waste, and minimization of its own environmental impact. In such ways, it contributes to the long term benefits to both the environment and local communities.

However, in the continuum of tourism activities that stretch from conventional tourism to ecotourism proper, there has been a lot of contention to the limit at which biodiversity preservation, local social-economic benefits, and environmental impact can be considered "ecotourism". For this reason, environmentalists, special interest groups, and governments define ecotourism differently. Environmental organizations have generally insisted that ecotourism is nature-based, sustainably managed, conservation supporting, and environmentally educated. The tourist industry and governments, however, focus more on the product aspect, treating ecotourism as equivalent to any sort of tourism based in nature. As a further complication, many terms are used under the rubric of ecotourism. Nature tourism, low impact tourism, green tourism, bio-tourism, ecologically responsible tourism, and others have been used in literature and marketing, although they are not necessary synonymous with ecotourism.

The problems associated with defining ecotourism have led to confusion among tourists and academics alike. Definitional problems are also subject of considerable public controversy and concern because of green washing, a trend towards the commercialization of tourism schemes disguised as sustainable, nature based, and environmentally friendly ecotourism. According to McLaren, these schemes are environmentally destructive, economically exploitative, and culturally insensitive at its worst. They are also morally disconcerting because they mislead tourists and manipulate their concerns for the environment. The development and success of such large scale, energy intensive, and ecologically unsustainable schemes are a testament to the tremendous profits associated with being labeled as ecotourism.

Negative Impact of Tourism

Ecotourism has become one of the fastest-growing sectors of the tourism industry, growing annually by 10-15% worldwide (Miller, 2007). One definition of ecotourism is "the practice of low-impact, educational, ecologically and culturally sensitive travel that benefits local communities and host countries" (Honey, 1999). Many of the ecotourism projects are not meeting these standards. Even if some of the guidelines are being executed, the local communities are still facing other negative impacts. South Africa is one of the countries that are reaping significant economic benefits from ecotourism, but negative effects - including forcing people to leave their homes, gross violations of fundamental rights, and environmental hazards - far outweigh the medium-term economic benefits (Miller, 2007). A tremendous amount of money is being spent and human resources continue to be used for ecotourism despite unsuccessful outcomes, and even more money is put into public relation campaigns to dilute the effects of criticism. Ecotourism channels resources away from other projects that could contribute more sustainable and realistic solutions to pressing social and environmental problems. "The money tourism can generate often ties parks and managements to eco-tourism" (Walpole et al. 2001). But there is a tension in this relationship because eco-tourism often causes conflict and changes in land-use rights, fails to deliver promises of community-level benefits, damages environments, and has plenty of other social impacts.

Indeed many argue repeatedly that eco-tourism is neither ecologically nor socially beneficial, yet it persists as a strategy for conservation and development (West, 2006). While several studies are being done on ways to improve the ecotourism structure, some argue that these examples provide rationale for stopping it altogether.

The ecotourism system exercises tremendous financial and political influence. The evidence above shows that a strong case exists for restraining such activities in certain locations. Funding could be used for field studies aimed at finding alternative solutions to tourism and the diverse problems Africa faces in result of urbanization, industrialization, and the over exploitation of agriculture (Kamuaro, 2007). At the local level, ecotourism has become a source of conflict over control of land, resources, and tourism profits. In this case, ecotourism has harmed the environment and local people, and has led to conflicts over profit distribution. In a perfect world more efforts would be made towards educating tourists of the environmental and social effects of their travels. Very few regulations or laws stand in place as boundaries for the investors in ecotourism. These should be implemented to prohibit the promotion of unsustainable ecotourism projects and materials which project false images of destinations, demeaning local and indigenous cultures.

Direct Environmental Impacts

Ecotourism operations occasionally fail to live up to conservation ideals. It is sometimes overlooked that ecotourism is a highly consumer-centered activity, and that environmental conservation is a means to further economic growth.

Although ecotourism is intended for small groups, even a modest increase in population, however temporary, puts extra pressure on the local environment and necessitates the development of additional infrastructure and amenities. The construction of water treatment plants, sanitation facilities, and lodges come with the exploitation of non-renewable energy sources and the utilization of already limited local resources. The conversion of natural land to such tourist infrastructure is implicated in deforestation and habitat deterioration of butterflies in Mexico and squirrel monkeys in Costa Rica. In other cases, the environment suffers because local communities are unable to meet the infrastructure demands of ecotourism. The lack of adequate sanitation facilities in many East African parks results in the disposal of campsite sewage in rivers, contaminating the wildlife, livestock, and people who draw drinking water from it.

Aside from environmental degradation with tourist infrastructure, population pressures from ecotourism also leaves behind garbage and pollution associated with the Western lifestyle. Although ecotourists claim to be educationally sophisticated and environmentally concerned, they rarely understand the ecological consequences of their visits and how their day-to-day activities append physical impacts on the environment. As one scientist observes, they "rarely acknowledge how the meals they eat, the toilets they flush, the water they drink, and so on, are all part of broader regional economic and ecological systems they are helping to reconfigure with their very activities." Nor do ecotourists recognize the great consumption of non-renewable energy required to arrive at their destination, which is typically more remote than conventional tourism destinations. For instance, an exotic journey to a place 10,000 kilometers away consumes about 700 liters of fuel per person.

Ecotourism activities are, in of itself, issues in environmental impact because they disturb fauna and flora. Ecotourists believe that because they are only taking pictures and leaving footprints, they keep ecotourism sites pristine, but even harmless sounding activities such as a nature hike can be ecologically destructive. In the Annapurna Circuit in Nepal, ecotourists have worn down the marked trails and created alternate routes, contributing to soil impaction, erosion, and plant damage. Where the ecotourism activity involves wildlife viewing, it can scare away animals, disrupt their feeding and nesting sites, or acclimate them to the presence of people. In Kenya, wildlife-observer disruption drives cheetahs off their reserves, increasing the risk of inbreeding and further endangering the species.

Environmental Hazards

The industrialization, urbanization, and unsustainable agriculture practices of human society are considered to be having a serious effect on the environment. Ecotourism is now also considered to be playing a role in this depletion. While the term ecotourism may sound relatively benign, one of its most serious impacts is its consumption of virgin territories (Kamuaro, 2007). These invasions often include deforestation, disruption of ecological life systems and various forms of pollution, all of which contribute to environmental degradation. The number of motor vehicles crossing the park increases as tour drivers search for rare species. The number of roads has disrupted the grass cover which has serious effects on plant and animal species. These areas also have a higher rate of disturbances and invasive species because of all the traffic moving off the beaten path into new undiscovered areas (Kamuaro, 2007). Ecotourism also has an effect on species through the value placed on them. "Certain species have gone from being little known or valued by local people to being highly valued commodities. The commodification of plants may erase their social value and lead to overproduction within protected areas. Local people and their images can also be turned into commodities" (West, 2006). Kamuaro brings up a relatively obvious contradiction, any commercial venture into unspoiled, pristine land with or without the "eco" prefix as a contradiction in terms. To generate revenue you have to have a high number of traffic, tourists, which inevitably means a higher pressure on the environment.

Local People

Most forms of ecotourism are owned by foreign investors and corporations that provide few benefits to local communities. An overwhelming majority of profits are put into the pockets of investors instead of reinvestment into the local economy or environmental protection. The limited numbers of local people who are employed in the economy enter at its lowest level, and are unable to live in tourist areas because of meager wages and a two market system.

In some cases, the resentment by local people results in environmental degradation. As a highly publicized case, the Masai nomads in Kenya killed wildlife in national parks to show aversion to unfair compensation terms and displacement from traditional lands. The lack of economic opportunities for local people also constrains them to degrade the environment as a means of sustenance. The presence of affluent ecotourists encourage the development of destructive markets in wildlife souvenirs, such as the sale of coral trinkets on tropical islands and animal products in Asia, contributing to illegal harvesting and poaching from the environment. In Suriname, sea turtle reserves use a very large portion of their budget to guard against these destructive activities.

Displacement of People

One of the most powerful examples of communities being moved in order to create a park is the story of the Masai. About 70% of national parks and game reserves in East Africa are on Masai land (Kamuaro, 2007). The first undesirable impact of tourism was that of the extent of land lost from the Masai culture. Local and national governments took advantage of the Masai's ignorance on the situation and robbed them of huge chunks of grazing land, putting to risk their only socio-economic livelihood. In Kenya the Masai also have not gained any economic benefits. Despite the loss of their land, employment favours better educated workers. Furthermore the investors in this area are not local and have not put profits back into local economy. In some cases game reserves can be created without informing or consulting local people, who come to find out about the situation when an eviction notice is delivered (Kamuaro, 2007). Another source of resentment is the manipulation of the local people by their government. "Eco-tourism works to create simplistic images of local people and their uses and understandings of their surroundings. Through the lens of these simplified images, officials direct policies and projects towards the local people and the local people are blamed if the projects fail" (West, 2006). Clearly tourism as a trade is not empowering the local people who make it rich and satisfying. Instead ecotourism exploits and depletes, particularly in African Masai tribes. It has to be reoriented if it is to be useful to local communities and to become sustainable (Kamuaro, 2007).

Threats to Indigenous Cultures

Ecotourism often claims that it preserves and "enhances" local cultures. However, evidence shows that with the establishment of protected areas local people have illegally lost their homes, and most often with no compensation (Kamuaro, 2007). Pushing people onto marginal lands with harsh climates, poor soils, lack of water, and infested with livestock and disease does little to enhance livelihoods even when a proportion of ecotourism profits are directed back into the community. The establishment of parks can create harsh survival realities and deprive the people of their traditional use of land and natural resources. Ethnic groups are increasingly being seen as a "backdrop" to the scenery and wildlife. The local people struggle for cultural survival and freedom of cultural expression while being "observed" by tourists. Local indigenous people also have strong resentment towards the change, "Tourism has been allowed to develop with virtually no controls. Too many lodges have been built, too much firewood is being used and no limits are being placed on tourism vehicles. They regularly drive off-track and harass the wildlife. Their vehicle tracks criss-cross the entire Masai Mara. Inevitably the bush is becoming eroded and degraded" (Kamuaro, 2007).

Mismanagement

While governments are typically entrusted with the administration and enforcement of environmental protection, they often lack the commitment or capability to manage ecotourism sites effectively. The regulations for environmental protection may be vaguely defined, costly to implement, hard to enforce, and uncertain in effectiveness. Government regulatory agencies, as political bodies, are susceptible to making decisions that spend budget on politically beneficial but environmentally unproductive projects. Because of prestige and conspicuousness, the construction of an attractive visitor's center at an ecotourism site may take precedence over more pressing environmental concerns like acquiring habitat, protecting endemic species, and removing invasive ones. Finally, influential groups can pressure and sway the interests of the government to their favor. The government and its regulators can become vested in the benefits of the ecotourism industry which they are supposed to regulate, causing restrictive environmental regulations and enforcement to become more lenient.

Management of ecotourism sites by private ecotourism companies offers an alternative to the cost of regulation and deficiency of government agencies. It is believed that these companies have a self interest in limited environmental degradation, because tourists will pay more for pristine environments, which translates to higher profit. However, theory indicates that this practice is not economically feasible and will fail to manage the environment.

The model of monopolistic competition states that distinctiveness will entail profits, but profits will promote imitation. A company that protects its ecotourism sites is able to charge a premium for the novel experience and pristine environment. But when other companies view the success of this approach, they also enter the market with similar practices, increasing competition and reducing demand. Eventually, the demand will be reduced until the economic profit is zero. A cost-benefit analysis shows that the company bears the cost of environmental protection without receiving the gains. Without economic incentive, the whole premise of self interest through environmental protection is quashed; instead, ecotourism companies will minimize environment related expenses and maximize tourism demand.

The tragedy of the commons offers another model for economic unsustainability from environmental protection, in ecotourism sites utilized by many companies. Although there is a communal incentive to protect the environment, maximizing the benefits in the long run, a company will conclude that it is in their best interest to utilize the ecotourism site beyond its sustainable level. By increasing the number of ecotourists, for instance, a company gains all the economic benefit while paying only a part of the environmental cost. In the same way, a company recognizes that there is no incentive to actively protect the environment; they bear all the costs, while the benefits are shared by all other companies. The result, again, is mismanagement.

Taken together, the mobility of foreign investment and lack of economic incentive for environmental protection means that ecotourism companies are disposed to establishing themselves in new sites once their existing one is sufficiently degraded.

Improving Sustainability

Regulation and Accreditation

Because the regulation of ecotourism is poorly implemented or nonexistent, ecologically destructive greenwashed operations like underwater hotels, helicopter tours, and wildlife theme parks are categorized as ecotourism along with canoeing, camping, photography, and wildlife observation. The failure to acknowledge responsible, low impact ecotourism puts these companies at a competitive disadvantage.

Many environmentalists have argued for a global standard of accreditation, differentiating ecotourism companies based on their level of environmental commitment. A national or international regulatory board would enforce accreditation procedures, with representation from various groups including governments, hotels, tour operators, travel agents, guides, airlines, local authorities, conservation organizations, and non-governmental organizations. The decisions of the board would be sanctioned by governments, so that non-compliant companies would be legally required to disassociate themselves from the use of the ecotourism brand.

Crinion suggests a Green Stars System, based on criteria including a management plan, benefit for the local community, small group interaction, education value and staff training. Ecotourists who consider their choices would be confident of a genuine ecotourism experience when they see the higher star rating.

In addition, environmental impact assessments could be used as a form of accreditation. Feasibility is evaluated from a scientific basis, and recommendations could be made to optimally plan infrastructure, set tourist capacity, and manage the ecology. This form of accreditation is more sensitive to site specific conditions.

Guidelines and education

An environmental protection strategy must address the issue of ecotourists removed from the cause-and-effect of their actions on the environment. More initiatives should be carried out to improve their awareness, sensitize them to environmental issues, and care about the places they visit.

Tour guides are an obvious and direct medium to communicate awareness. With the confidence of ecotourists and intimate knowledge of the environment, they can actively discuss conservation issues. A tour guide training program in Costa Rica's Tortuguero National Park has helped mitigate negative environmental impacts by providing information and regulating tourists on the parks' beaches used by nesting endangered sea turtles.

Small scale, slow growth and local control

The underdevelopment theory of tourism describes a new form of imperialism by multinational corporations that control ecotourism resources. These corporations finance and profit from the development of large scale ecotourism that causes excessive environmental degradation, loss of traditional culture and way of life, and exploitation of local labor. In Zimbabwe and Nepal's Annapurna region, where underdevelopment is taking place, more than 90 percent of ecotourism revenues are expatriated to the parent countries, and less than 5 percent go into local communities.

The lack of sustainability highlights the need for small scale, slow growth, and locally based ecotourism. Local peoples have a vested interest in the well being of their community, and are therefore more accountable to environmental protection than multinational corporations. The lack of control, westernization, adverse impacts to the environment, loss of culture and traditions outweigh the benefits of establishing large scale ecotourism.

The increased contributions of communities to locally managed ecotourism create viable economic opportunities, including high level management positions, and reduce environmental issues associated with poverty and unemployment. Because the ecotourism experience is marketed to a different lifestyle from large scale ecotourism, the development of facilities and infrastructure does not need to conform to corporate Western tourism standards, and can be much simpler and less expensive. There is a greater multiplier effect on the economy, because local products, materials, and labor are used. Profits accrue locally and import leakages are reduced. However, even this form of tourism may require foreign investment for promotion or start up. When such investments are required, it is crucial for communities for find a company or non-governmental organization that reflects the philosophy of ecotourism; sensitive to their concerns and willing to cooperate at the expense of profit. The basic assumption of the multiplier effect is that the economy starts off with unused resources, for example, that many workers are cyclically unemployed and much of industrial capacity is sitting idle or incompletely utilized. By increasing demand in the economy it is then possible to boost production. If the economy was already at full employment, with only structural, frictional, or other supply-side types of unemployment, any attempt to boost demand would only lead to inflation. For various laissez-faire schools of economics which embrace Say's Law and deny the possibility of Keynesian inefficiency and under-employment of resources, therefore, the multiplier concept is irrelevant or wrong-headed.

As an example, consider the government increasing its expenditure on roads by $one million, without a corresponding increase in taxation. This sum would go to the road builders, who would hire more workers and distribute the money as wages and profits. The households receiving these incomes will save part of the money and spend the rest on consumer goods. These expenditures in turn will generate more jobs, wages, and profits, and so on with the income and spending circulating around the economy.

The multiplier effect arises because of the induced increases in consumer spending which occur due to the increased incomes - and because of the feedback into increasing business revenues, jobs, and income again. This process does not lead to an economic explosion not only because of the supply-side barriers at potential output (full employment) but because at each "round", the increase in consumer spending is less than the increase in consumer incomes. That is, the marginal propensity to consume (mpc) is less than one, so that each round some extra income goes into saving, leaking out of the cumulative process. Each increase in spending is thus smaller than that of the previous round, preventing an explosion.Ecotourism has to be implemented with care.

Natural Resource Management

Natural resource management can be utilized as a specialized tool for the development of eco-tourism. There are several places throughout the world where the amount of natural resources are abundant. But, with human encroachment and habitats these resources are depleting. Without knowing the proper utilization of certain resources they are destroyed and floral and faunal species are becoming extinct. Ecotourism programmes can be introduced for the conservation of these resources. Several plans and proper management programmes can be introduced so that these resources remain untouched. Several organizations, NGO's, scientists are working on this field.

Natural resources of hill areas like Kurseong in West Bengal are plenty in number with various flora and fauna, but tourism for business purpose poised the situation. Researcher from Jadavpur University presently working in this area for the develeopment of eco-tourism which can be utilized as a tool for natural resource management.

In South-East Asia government and Non-Government Organisations are working together with academics and industry operators to spread the economic benefits of tourism into the kampungs and villages of the region. A recently formed alliance, the South-East Asian Tourism Organisation - SEATO is bringing together these diverse players to allay resource management concerns

Silent Valley National Park (Core zone: 236.74 square kilometres (91 sq mi)) is located in the Nilgiri Hills, Palakkad District in Kerala, South India. The area in this national park was historically explored in 1847 by the botanist Robert Wight, and is associated with Hindu legend. .

The park is one of the last undisturbed tracts of South Western Ghats montane rain forests and tropical moist evergreen forest in India. Contiguous with the proposed Karimpuzha National Park (225 km^2) to the north and Mukurthi National Park (78.46 km^2) to the north-east, it is the core of the Nilgiri International Biosphere Reserve (1,455.4 km^2), and is part of The Western Ghats World Heritage Site, Nilgiri Sub-Cluster (6,000+ km^2) under consideration by UNESCO.

Plans for a hydroelectric project that threatened the parks high diversity of wildlife stimulated an environmentalist Social Movement in the 1970s called Save Silent Valley which resulted in cancellation of the project and creation of the park in 1980. The visitors' centre for the park is at Sairandhri.

The area is locally known as "Sairandhrivanam" literally, in Malayalam: Sairandhri's Forest. In local Hindu legend, Sairandhri is Draupadi, the polyandrous wife of the five Pandavas, who disguised herself as Sairandhri, queen Sudeshna's assistant, while they were in exile. The Pandavas, deprived of their kingdom, set out on a 13-year exile. They wandered south, into what is now Kerala, until one day they came upon a magical valley where rolling grasslands met wooded ravines, a deep green river bubbled its course through impenetrable forest, where at dawn and twilight the tiger and elephant would drink together at the water's edge, where all was harmonious and man unknown. Beside that river, in a cave on a hill slope, the Pandavas halted.

English Exploration

The first English investigation of the watersheds of the Silent Valley area was in 1847 by the botanist Robert Wight.

The British named the area Silent Valley because of a perceived absence of noisy Cicadas. Another story attributes the name to the anglicisation of Sairandhri. A third story, refers to the presence there of many Lion-Tailed Macaques Macaca silenus. In 1914 the forest of the Silent Valley area was declared a Reserve Forest, however, from 1927 to 1976 portions of the Silent Valley forest area were subjected to forestry operations. In 1928 the location on the Kunthipuzha River at Sairandhri was identified as an ideal site for electricity generation and in 1958 a study and survey of the area was conducted and a hydroelectric project of 120 MV costing Rs. 17 Crore was proposed by the Kerala State Electricity Board.

Environmental Concerns

Silent Valley is home to the largest population of Lion-tailed Macaque, an endangered species of Primate. Public controversy over their habitat led to establishment of Silent Valley National Park.

In 1973 the valley became the focal point of "Save Silent Valley", India's fiercest environmental debate of the decade, when the Kerala State Electricity Board decided to implement the Silent Valley Hydro-Electric Project (SVHEP) centered on a dam across the Kunthipuzha River. The resulting reservoir would flood 8.3 km^2 of virgin rainforest and threaten the Lion-tailed Macaque. In 1976 the Kerala State Electricity Board announced plans to begin dam construction and the issue was brought to public attention. Romulus Whitaker, founder of the Madras Snake Park and the Madras Crocodile Bank, was probably the first person to draw public attention to the small and remote area.

In 1983 the Honorable Prime Minister of India, Indira Gandhi, decided to abandon the Project and on November 15 the Silent Valley forests were declared as a National Park. On September 7, 1985 the Silent Valley National Park was formally inaugurated and a memorial at Sairandhri to Indira Gandhi was unveiled by Shri. Rajiv Gandhi, the new Hon. Prime Minister of

India. On September 1, 1986 Silent Valley National Park was designated as the core area of the Nilgiri Biosphere Reserve. Since then, a long-term conservation effort has been undertaken to preserve the Silent Valley ecosystem.

In 2001 a new hydro project was proposed and the "Man vs. Monkey debate" was revived. The proposed site of the dam (64.5 m high and 275 m long) is just 3.5 km downstream of the old dam site at Sairandhiri, 500 m outside the National Park boundary. The Kerala Minister for Electricity called The Pathrakkadavu dam (PHEP) an "eco-friendly alternative" to the old Silent Valley project. The claim was that the submergence area of the PHEP would be a negligible .041 km² compared to 8.30 km² submergence of the 1970s (SVHEP). During January to May 2003 a rapid Environmental Impact Assessment (EIA) was carried out. Little more was heard till November 15, 2006 when Kerala Minister for Forest Binoy Viswam said that the proposed buffer zone for Silent Valley would be declared soon.

On February 21, 2007 Chief Minister A. K. Antony told reporters after a cabinet meeting that "when the Silent Valley proposal was dropped, the centre had promised to give clearance to the Pooyamkutty project. This promise, however, had not been honoured. The Kerala government has not taken any decision on reviving the Silent Valley Hydel Project".

On April 18, 2007, Kerala Chief Minister V S Achuthanandan and his cabinet approved the Pathrakkadavu Hydro-electric project and sent it to the Union Government for environmental approval.

Buffer Zone

Territorial forests located around the national park have been subject to a working-plan to accomplish revenue oriented objectives such as extraction of bamboo and reed which affect the long-term conservation of the park. In addition Illegal activities such as ganja cultivation, setting forest fires, trapping and poaching wild animals, frequently occur in the territorial forests located in the immediate vicinity of the national park. This has resulted in degradation of habitat and reduced forest cover, which has adverse effects on the long term survival of the core area of the national park.

On November 21, 2009, Union Minister of Forest and Environment Jairam Ramesh and Kerala Forest Minister Binoy Viswam declared, while inaugurating the silver jubilee celebration of Silent Valley National Park in Palakkad, that the buffer zone of the Park would be made an integral part of it in order to ensure better protection of the area. This means that the total park area is now increased to 236.74 square kilometres (91 sq mi).

On June 6, 2007 the Kerala cabinet approved the buffer zone proposal. The new 147.22 km^2 zone will include 80.75 km^2 taken from Attapady Forest Range, 27.09 km^2 from Mannarkkad Forest Range and 39.38 km^2 from Kalikavu Forest range and consolidated to form a new range, Bhavani Forest Range, of 94 km^2 and 54 km^2 would be brought under the existing Silent Valley Range of the National Park. The Cabinet also sanctioned 35 staff to protect the area and two new forest stations in Bhavani range at Anavai and Thudukki. Forest Minister Benoy Viswom said "the zone would have reserve forest status and tribals in the area would not be affected. The decision reaffirmed the commitment of the LDF Government to protection of environment. The zone is a necessity, not just of the State but also of the nation."

The proposal was then sent to Kerala Minister for Electricity, Mr. A.K. Balan, who has voiced the need for setting up the Pathrakadavu hydroelectric project in the proposed southwest buffer zone of the National Park, the Thenkara Range of the Mannarkkad Forest Division. As of May 9, 2007 Mr. Balan has not given his opinion on the buffer zone proposal.

In August 2006, the new Minister for Forests, Benoy Viswom, approved a proposal from the Conservator of Forests for a 148 km² buffer zone around the core area of the park. The proposal says: "It is felt absolutely essential that an effective buffer of forests should be immediately formed around the national park in order to save the world famous Silent Valley National Park from all potential dangers. This can only be achieved by bringing the management of Silent Valley National Park as well as the proposed buffer zone under one management umbrella to insulate the park from all possible dangers." The proposed buffer zone will have 94 km² in Attappady Reserve Forest east of the Kunthipuzha and 54 km² taken from the Mannarkaad range and Nilambur south division west of the river.

In January 2006, the former Kerala Minister for Forest and Environment, A. Sujanapal, said the Government would consider the demand for a 600 km² buffer zone for Silent Valley National Park made by Bharathapuzha Protection Committee, Malampuzha Protection Committee, One Earth One Life and Jana Jagratha. A buffer zone proposal was made in the 1986 park management plan but not implemented.

In 1979, Dr. M.S. Swaminathan, then Secretary to the Department of Agriculture, visited the Silent Valley area and suggested that 389.52 km² including the Silent Valley (89.52 km²), New Amarambalam (80 km²), Attappadi (120 km²) in Kerala and Kunda in Coimbatore (100 km²) reserve forests, should be developed into a National Rainforest Biosphere Reserve.

Geography

Silent Valley is rectangular, 7 km (east-west) X 12 km (north-south). Located between 11°03' to 11°13' N latitude and 76°21' to 76°35' E longitude it is separated from the eastern and northern high altitude plateaus of the (Nilgiris Mountains) by high continuous ridges including Sispara Peak (2,206 m) at the north end of the park. The park gradually slopes southward down to the Palakkad plains and to the west it is bounded by irregular ridges. The altitude of the park ranges from 658 m to 2328 m at Anginda Peak, but most of the park lies within the altitude range of 880 m to 1200 m. Soils are blackish and slightly acidic in evergreen forests where there is good accumulation of organic matter. The underlying rock in the area is granite with schists and gneiss, which give rise to the loamy laterite soils on slopes.

Rivers

The Kuntipuzha River drains the entire 15 km length of the park from north to south into the Bharathapuzha River. Kuntipuzha River divides the park into a narrow eastern sector of width 2 kilometers and a wide western sector of 5 kilometers. The river is characterized by its crystal clear and perennial nature. The main tributaries of the river, kunthancholapuzha, Karingathodu, Madrimaranthodu, Valiaparathodu and Kummaathanthodu originate on the upper slopes of the eastern side of the valley. The river is uniformly shallow, with no flood plains or meanders. Its bed falls from 1,861 m to 900 m over a distance of 12 km, the last 8 km being particularly level with a fall of only 60 m. Kuntipuzha is one of the less torrential rivers of the Western Ghats, with a pesticide-free catchment area.

Silent Valley gets copious amounts of rainfall during the monsoons, but the actual amount varies within the region due the varied topography. In general the rainfall is higher at higher altitude and decreases from the west to east due to the rain shadow effect. Eighty per cent of the rainfall occurs during the south-west monsoon between June and September. It also receives significant amount of rainfall during the north-east monsoon between October and November.

The park being completely enclosed within a ring of hills, has its own micro-climate and probably receives some convectional rainfall, in addition to rain from two monsoons. In the remaining months, condensation on vegetation of mist shrouding the valley is estimated to yield 15 per cent of the total water generated in the rainforest.

In 2006, the Walakkad area of the park received the highest ever annual rainfall of 9,569.6 mm. In 2000, the figure was 7,788 mm; in 2001, 8,351.9 mm; in 2004, 8465.3 mm; and in 2005, 9,347.8 mm. The annual rainfall received in the valley (at Sairandhri?) was 7,788.8 mm in 2000; 8,361.9 mm in 2001. In 2002, 4,262.5 mm; in 2003, 3,499.65 mm; in 2004, 6,521.27 mm, in 2005, 6,919.38 mm; in 2006, 6,845.05 mm; in 2007, 6,009.35 mm; and in 2008 it was 4386.5 mm. The figure till October 2009 was 5,477.4 mm. Average annual rainfall in the park between 2000 and 2008 was thus 6,066 mm.

The mean annual temperature is 20.2 °C. The hottest months are April and May when the mean temperature is 23 °C and the coolest months are January and February when the mean temperature is 18o C. Because of the high rainfall, the relative humidity is consistently high (above 95%) between June and December.

Tribes

There is no record the valley has ever been settled, but the Mudugar and Irula tribal people are indigenous to the area and do live in the adjacent valley of Attappady Reserved Forest. Also, the Kurumbar people occupy the highest range outside the park bordering on the Nilgiris.

Many of the Mudugar and Irula now work as day laborers and porters. Some work for the Forest Department in the park as forest guards and visitor guides. 16 out of 21 tribal colonies in the Attappady range are notorious for ganja cultivation. Many Mudugar are in abject poverty and easily recruited by the so called ganja mafia, There is a plan to employ 50 additional men from these 21 tribal settlements as forest guards for Rs.500/man/month.

Fauna and Flora

Valley areas of the park are in a Tropical and subtropical moist broadleaf forests Ecoregion. Hilly areas above 1,000 m are in a South Western Ghats montane rain forests region. Above 1,500 m, the evergreen forests begin to give way to stunted forests, called sholas, interspersed with open grassland. Both are very important to naturalists, biologists and other researchers because the rich biodiversity here has never been disturbed by human settlements. Several threatened species are endemic here. New plant and animal species are often discovered here.

Fauna

Birds

Birdlife International lists 16 bird species in Silent Valley as threatened or restricted: Nilgiri Wood-pigeon, Malabar Parakeet, Malabar Grey Hornbill, White-bellied Treepie, Grey-headed Bulbul, Broad-tailed Grassbird, Rufous Babbler, Wynaad Laughing Thrush, Nilgiri Laughing Thrush, White-bellied Shortwing, Black-and-rufous Flycatcher, Nilgiri Flycatcher, White-bellied Blue-flycatcher, Crimson-backed Sunbird and Nilgiri pipit.

Rare bird species found here include Ceylon Frogmouth and Great Indian Hornbill. The 2006 winter bird survey discovered Long-legged Buzzard, a new species of raptor at Sispara, the park's highest peak. The survey found 10 endangered species recorded in the IUCN Red List including the Red winged crested cuckoo, Malabar Pied Hornbill, Pale harrier. The area is home to 15 endemic species including the Black-and-orange Flycatcher. It recorded 138 species of birds including 17 species that were newly observed in the Silent Valley area. The most abundant bird was the Black bulbul.

Mammals

There are at least 34 species of mammals at Silent Valley including the threatened Lion-tailed Macaque, Niligiri Langur, Malabar Giant Squirrel, Nilgiri Tahr, Peshwa's Bat (Myotis peshwa) and Hairy-winged Bat. There are nine species of bats, rats and mice.

Distribution and demography of all diurnal primates were studied in Silent Valley National Park and adjacent areas for a period of three years from 1993 to 1996. Fourteen troops of lion-tailed macaque, eighty-five troops of Nilgiri langur, fifteen troops of bonnet macaque and seven troops of Hanuman langur were observed. Of these, the Nilgiri langur was randomly distributed, whereas the lion-tailed macaque troops were confined to the southern sector of the Park. Bonnet macaques and Hanuman langurs were occasional visitors. The Silent Valley forest remains one of the most undisturbed viable habitats left for the endemic and endangered primates lion-tailed macaque and Nilgiri langur.

The tiger, leopard (panther), leopard cat, jungle cat, fishing cat, Common Palm Civet, Small Indian Civet, Brown Palm Civet, Ruddy Mongoose, Stripe-necked Mongoose, Dhole, clawless otter, sloth bear, small travancore flying squirrel, Indian pangolin (scaly anteater), porcupine, wild boar, sambar, spotted deer, barking deer, mouse deer and gaur also live here.

Insects

There are at least 730 identified species of insects in the park. The maximum number of species belong to the orders Lepidoptera and Coleoptera. Many unclassified species have been collected and there is a need for further studies.

33 species of crickets and grasshoppers have been recorded of which one was new. 39 species of true bugs (six new) and two species of Homoptera (both new) have been recorded. 128 species of beetles including 10 new species have been recorded.

Over 128 species of butterflies and 400 species of moths live here. A 1993 study found butterflies belonging to 9 families. The families Nymphalidae and Papilionidae contained the maximum number of species. 13 species were endemic to South India, including 5 species having protected status. 7 species of Butterflies were observed migrating in a mixed swarm of thousands of butterflies towards the Silent Valley National Park. In one instance an observer noted several birds attempting to catch these butterflies. The bird species included the Pied Bushchat Saxicola caprata, Nilgiri Pipit Anthus nilghiriensis, Tickell's Warbler Phylloscopus affinis, Greenish Leaf-Warbler Phylloscopus trochiloides and the Oriental White-eye Zosterops palpebrosa.

At least 500 species of earthworms and leeches have also been identified in the park.

Flora

The flora of the valley include about a 1000 species of flowering plants, 108 species of orchids, 100 ferns and fern allies, 200 liverworts, 75 lichens and about 200 algae. A majority Of these plants are endemic to the Western Ghats.

In addition to facilitating recharge of the aquifer, water retention of the catchment basin and preventing soil erosion, every plant in the park from the smallest one celled algae to the largest tree in the forest has unknown potential for beneficial innovations in biotechnology.

Flowering Plants

Angiosperm flora currently identified here include 966 species belonging to 134 families and 599 genera. There are 701 Dicotyledons distributed among 113 families and 420 genera. There are 265 Monocotyledons here distributed among 21 families and 139 genera. Families best represented are the Orchids with 108 species including the rare, endemic and highly endangered orchids Ipsea malabarica, Bulbophyllum silentvalliensis and Eria tiagii, Grasses (56), Legumes (55), Rubiaceae (49) and Asters (45). There are many rare, endemic and economically valuable species, such as cardamom Ellettaria cardamomum, black pepper Piper nigrum, yams Dioscorea spp., beans Phaseolus sp., a pest-resistant strain of rice Oryza Pittambi, and 110 plant species of importance in Ayurvedic medicine. Seven new plant species have been recorded from Silent Valley, including in 1996, Impatiens sivarajanii, a new species of Balsaminaceae.

Trees

Occurrence of lion-tailed macaque is dependent on the flowering of Cullenia exarillata in the forest.

Six distinct tree associations have been described in the valley. Three are restricted to the southern sector: (Cullenia exarillata & Palaquium ellipticum), (Palaquium ellipticum & Mesua ferrea(Indian rose chestnut) and (Mesua ferrea & Calophyllum elatum). The remainder are confined to the central and northern parts of the Park: (Palaquium ellipticum & Poeciloneuron indicum), (Calophyllum elatum & Ochlandra sp.) and (Poeciloneuron indicum & Ochlandra sp.).

A study of natural regeneration of 12 important tree species of Silent Valley tropical rain forests showed good natural regeneration of all 12 species. The species studied were Palaquium ellipticum, Cullenia exarillata, Poeciloneuron indicum, Myristica dactyloides, Elaeocarpus glandulosus, Litsea floribunda, Mesua nagassarium, Cinnamomum malabatrum, Agrostistachys meeboldii, Calophyllum polyanthum, Garcinia morella and Actinodaphne campanulata.

Recent selective felling of three trees per acre, has led to the cutting of 48,000 m^3 of timber from about 20 km^2.

There is a huge hollow Kattualying tree here which can fit 12 people inside.

Genetic Resources

Throughout human history about 10% of the genetic stock found in the wild has been bred into palatable and higher yielding cereals, fruits and vegetables. Future food security depends on the preservation of the remaining 90% of the stock through protection of high biodiversity habitats like Silent valley.

The National Bureau of Plant Genetic Resources of ICAR (India), Plant Exploration and Collection Division has identified Silent Valley as high in bio-diversity and an important Gene Pool resource for Recombinant DNA innovations. An important example of use of wild germplasm is gene selection from the wild varieties of rice Oryza nivara (Central India) and Oryza Pittambi found in Silent Valley for the traits of broad spectrum disease resistance in high yielding hybrid rice varieties including IR-36, which are responsible for much of the green revolution throughout Asia.

Also, genetic evaluation of plant growth promoting Rhizobacteria obtained from Silent Valley indicated that strain, IISR 331, could increase the growth of black pepper cuttings by 228% and showed 82.7% inhibition of the common plant wilting disease Phytopthora capsici in laboratory tests (in vitro).

Challenges

Forest Fire

Fire is one of the major threats facing the forests of Kerala. People engaged in grazing livestock often burn an area to get fresh grass shoots for their cattle, especially during dry season when fire danger is greatest. Also, illicit activities like ganja cultivation, poaching, tree felling, non'timber forest products (NTFP) collection and very often careless tourists and pilgrims are responsible for big forest fires. Some extent of the Mesua - Calophyllum tree association areas in the higher reaches are degraded due to previous fire and the area is now fast regenerating.

Cannabis cultivation

The cannabis mafia has cut hundreds of acres of evergreen tropical forest in the Attappady Hills, including Silent Valley buffer zones, for illegal cultivation of the cash crop. The Forest Department had an ambitious plan to root out ganja cultivation from the Attappady forests by April 2006.

Dudhwa National Park is located in the Terai of Uttar Pradesh, India and covers an area of 680 km2 with a buffer area of almost 190 km2. The Park was created thanks to the efforts of 'Billy' Arjan Singh, who fought for the protection of the animals he loved. The area was established in 1958 as a wildlife sanctuary, February 1, 1977 as a national park and 1988 as a tiger reserve. Dudhwa Tiger Reserve lies on the India-Nepal border in the foothills of the Himalaya.

Headquarters : Lakhimpur Kheri District, UP, India

Altitude: 150-183 meters Nearest Town: Palia (10 km.) Nearest petrol pump! Hospital / market /bank / Post & Telegraph Office are at Palia

While the northern edge of the Park lies along the Indo-Nepal border, the River Suheli is in the southern boundary.

Climate

Like the rest of north India, Dudhwa also has an extreme type of climate. Summers are hot with the temperature rising up to 40 °C. During winters, the temperature hovers between 20 and 30 °C. The average annual rainfall is 1,600 mm.

Mid November-mid June, the best period being February-April.

Vegetation

Dudhwa National Park is full of mosaic grasslands and dense sal forests to swampy marshes.

The Dudhwa National Park is punctuated by extensive stretches of grasslands. The predominant tree species found in the park are Shorea robusta, Terminalis tomentosa, Adina cordifolia, Eugenia jambolana, Terminalia belerica, Bombax malabaricum and Dalbergia sissoo, and more.

The forests here are reminiscent of the forests of Bardia on the Nepal side, with huge Sal trees, tall termite mounds, patches of riverine forests and large open grasslands. Its lakes offer excellent opportunities for observing Swamp Deer, Hog Deer, and birds from 'machans'.

Dudhwa National Park is home to one of the finest Sal forests in India, some of these trees are more than 150 years old and over 70 feet tall. In 1976, the park had a population of 50 tigers, 41 elephants and 76 bears apart from five species of deer, more than 400 species of birds, crocodiles and some other species of mammals and reptiles. its a very near to capital(lucknow).

Fauna

Some rare species inhabit the park. Hispid Hare, earlier thought to have become extinct, was rediscovered in 1984.

In the mid 1980s, Indian Rhinoceros was reintroduced into Dudhwa from Assam and Nepal.

The other animals to be seen here include Swamp Deer, Sambar Deer, Barking Deer, Spotted Deer, Hog Deer, Tiger, Rhinoceros, Sloth Bear, Ratel, Jackal, Civet, Jungle Cat, Fishing Cat, Leopard Cat.

The major attractions of Dudhwa National Park are the Tigers and Swamp Deer. The main attractions of the park are its Swamp Deer (population over 1,600) and tiger (population 98 in 1995). The park is famous for the efforts of 'Billy' Arjan Singh, one of India's leading conservationists, who was instrumental in the creation of Dudhwa as a sanctuary of the Swamp Deer. Later he successfully hand-reared and re-introduced zoo-born tigers and leopards into the wilds of Dudhwa.

The park has a rich bird life, with over 350 species, including the Swamp Francolin, Great Slaty Woodpecker and Bengal Florican. Dudhwa also boasts a range of migratory birds that settle here during winters. It includes among others, painted storks, black and white necked storks, Sarus Cranes, woodpeckers, barbets, kingfishers, minivans, bee-eaters, bulbuls and varied night birds of prey.

Dudwa National Park is a stronghold of the barasingha, which can be spotted in herds of hundreds. It is interesting to note that around half of the world's barasinghas are present in Dudhwa National Park. Smaller than the sambar, the barasinghas have 12 antlers that collectively measure up to 100 cm.

Barasinghas: Passing through open grasslands, one can spot herd of these rare animals. Around half of the surviving population of Barasinghas is found in the park. These animals are smaller than sambar and weigh around 180 kg. The barasinghas have 12 antlers that measure up to 100 cm. Due to their slightly woolly, dark brown to pale yellow cloak, the grasslands acts as the perfect camouflage.

Birds

Drongos, Barbets, Cormorants, Ducks, Geese, Hornbills, Bulbuls, Teal, Woodpeckers, Heron, Bee Eaters, Minivets, Kingfishers, Egrets, Orioles, plenty of painted storks, sarus cranes, owls and more. One can also spot rare species like the Bengal florican.

Dudhwa's birds in particular are a delight for any avid bird watcher. The marshlands are habitat for about 400 species of resident and migratory birds including the Swamp Francolin, Great Slaty Woodpecker, Bengal Florican, plenty of Painted Stork, Sarus Crane, several species of owl, Asian barbet, woodpecker and minivets. Much of the park's avian fauna is aquatic in nature and found around Dudhwa's lakes such as Banke Tal.

Tourist Attractions

En route to Dudhwa, the unique Frog Temple at Oyal can also be visited. The only one of its kind in India, it was built by the former Maharajas of the Oyal state in the district of Lakhimpur-Kheri. Dedicated to Lord Shiva, the base of the stone temple is built in the shape of a large frog. The temple is at a distance of 10 km from Hargaon on the route to Lakhimpur-Kheri and Dudhwa.

Surat Bhawan Palace

Built in the Indo-Saracenic style by the rulers of the Singhai state, Surat Bhawan Palace is one of the famous palaces of the Terai area. Not far from the Dudhwa Tiger Reserve on the Lakhimpur-Nighasan-Dudhwa route, the palace is set in a large green, 9-acre (36,000 m2) retreat. Expanses of lush lawns, fountains, a swimming pool and interesting architectural details make a visit to the palace worthwhile.

Frog Temple: This temple, dedicated to Lord Shiva, is located in Oyal, which is nearly 10 km from Hurgaon en route Lakhimpur-Kheri. The base of the temple is in the shape of a large frog.

Surat Bhawan Palace: This 19th century Indo-Sarasenic style built Palace is located around 8 km from the Dudhwa National Park. One can see the Himalayan Peaks from the Palace terrace on a clear day.

Indian Elephant

Elephant Rides: The spotting of animals and birds in their natural habitation, and that too sitting on top of an Indian elephant is an experience to treasure for a long time.

dudhwalive.com is an e-magazine of wildlife news and environmental issues. The dudhwalive is the most popular wildlife in India and other Countries, where people like environmental news in their own mother tongue. This website is broadcast on All India Radio and on various news channels of India. The contents of this e-magazine are regularly publish in newspapers and magazines. Actually dudhwalive is a large network of websites including such as dudhwalive channel, Jungle Katha, Manhan Village, Dudhwa and Nukoosh-e-Kataran.

Travel Information

Drive from Delhi (8-9 hours) or take the train to Shahjehanpur and drive to Dudhwa (3 hours). Alternatively fly to Lucknow and drive to Dudhwa (245 km, 6 hours).

Nearest Railway Station: Dudwa (4 km.), Palia (10 km.), Mailani (37 km.) Nearest Airport: Lucknow, Dhangarhi (Nepal, 35 km.).

Namdapha National Park is the largest protected area in the Eastern Himalaya biodiversity hotspot and is located in Arunachal Pradesh in Northeast India. It is also the largest national park in India in terms of area. It is located in the Eastern Himalayan sub-region and is recognized as one of the richest areas in biodiversity in India . The park harbours the northernmost lowland evergreen rainforests in the world at 27°N latitude . The area is also known for extensive Dipterocarp forests.

The park is located in Changlang district of the Northeastern state of Arunachal Pradesh, near its border with Myanmar. It spans an area of 1985 km2 with 177 km2 in buffer zone and 1808 km2 in the core area. The park is located between the Dapha bum range of the Mishmi Hills and the Patkai range with a wide altitudinal range between 200 m asl and 4571 m asl . The area falls under both the Palearctic and Indo Malayan biogeographic areas resulting in a diverse species assemblage. The habitat changes with increasing altitude from sub-tropical broadleaved forests to subtropical pine forests, temperate broadleaved forests and at the higher elevations, to alpine meadows and perennial snow. The park has extensive bamboo and secondary forests in addition to the primary forests.

Because of many different vegetation zones, the park is home to a great diversity of mammal species. Four big cat species occurre in the park: snow leopards, clouded leopards, common leopards and tigers. Other large predators are dholes, wolves, and Asiatic black bears. Smaller carnivores include red panda, red fox, yellow-throated marten, Eurasian otter, Oriental small-clawed otter, spotted linsang, binturong, common palm civet, small indian civet, large indian civet, masked palm civet, marbled cat, fishing cat, Asiatic golden cat, and two species of mongoose. Large herbivores are represented by elephants wild boar, forest musk deer, indian muntjac, hog deer, sambar, gaur, common goral, mainland serow, takin and bharal . Seven species of non-human primates including Stump-tailed macaque and Slow Loris, Hoolock Gibbons, Capped Langurs, Assamese Macaques and Rhesus Macaques.

Birds

Namdapha has about 425 bird species with many more to be recorded from work in the higher areas . There are five species of Hornbills recorded from the area. Several species of rare wren-babblers have been recorded in Namdapha. Other bird groups include laughing thrushes, parrotbills, fulvettas, shrike babblers and scimitar babblers. The Snowythroated Babbler is a rare species of Babbler found only in the Patkai and Mishmi hills and nearby areas in Northern Myanmar, is found in Namdapha. Other rare, restricted range or globally endangered species include the White-bellied Heron, Rufous-necked Hornbill, Green Cochoa, Purple Cochoa, Beautiful Nuthatch, Ward's Trogon, Ruddy Kingfisher, Blue-eared Kingfisher, Whitetailed fish eagle, Eurasian Hobby, Pied Falconet, White-winged Wood Duck, Himalayan Wood-owl, Rufous-throated Hill-partridge, and Whitecheeked hill partridge. Several leaf warblers and migrants such as Amur Falcon and several Thrushes can be seen here.

Ethnography

There are a few settlements of Lisu tribal people within the park. Most of the Lisus are, however, located beyond the eastern border of the park towards the international border of India with Myanmar. There are also Chakma, Tangsa and Singpho settlements around the park.

Eco-Tourism in Australia

Base: Gold Coast

Ecology and protection of the environment does not lack in Australia. Fines can be severe for those who do not follow Australia's rules of preservation. All that should be taken away from national parks and marine parks are photographs and any garbage, including cigarette buds. Any fires lit need to be treated with great attention, and make sure that the fire has been put out well when finished. In some forest, marine parks, and islands, it is necessary to get permission (normally by buying a permit). If you want to camp, prices for such permits are very low, and is in place more as a form of control. Consult the Rangers about any type of activity you intend to make, either in a marine park, reserve forest, or any national parks. Remember there are many types of animals that can present some danger such as snakes, spiders, and even poisonous plants.

There are more than a thousand National Parks in Australia, all kept by the rangers, and are well marked. Most of the parks offer simple and free maps, and some parks have detailed maps for sale, prices ranging from A$10. Many parks have Aborigines relics that are considered sacred, and the destruction of any form, could pose heavy fines and even prison. Australia has all types of parks. They include some deserts, sub-tropical, tropical vegetation, Marine Parks etc. The number is so large that it would be almost impossible to describe each one. If you would like to know more about it, there is a guide in bookstores, with tips and description of most parks.

On the Gold Coast the main National Parks are the following:

Lamington National Park - 20.600 hectares of valleys and green hills covered by rainforest. This park is divided in two sections: Binna Burra and Green Mountains. There are many tracks for all kinds of bushwalkers and ages, with a great variety of birds, native animals and caves to be observed and appreciated.

Mt Barney National Park - Most of the area is covered by Eucalyptus, however there are also areas with forest, waterfalls, valleys, and diversified rare plants. Phone: 54635041

Springbrook National Park - This park is only 40 km from the Gold Coast, enclosed in the mountains which surrounds the city, this place is perfect for a picnic with family or friends. The park has beautiful vegetation, and an abundance of wildlife. There are tracks leading you to the edge of the mountain, and even underneath waterfalls. Lookout points offer wonderful views of the Tweed Valley, Surfers Paradise, and most of the Gold Coast. The park is a remnant part of an extinct volcano, Mt.Warning, which is the highest peak in the area. The Natural Arch (photo) is one of the greatest attractions.

Numinbah Valley - Between the Lamington and the Springbrook Parks, this place has its own "Natural Bridge", a natural bridge with waterfall. At night, the cave is illuminated by a large colony of "Glow-worms" (species of firefly that does not blink and are always glowing).

Mc Pherson Ranges - It's located in southern Gold Coast, crossing the border to the state of New South Wales, and following west in direction of the colourful city of Murwillumbah, near the Tweed River. Amongst the best activities, are climbing Mt.Warning and bush walking through the various challenging tracks.

Tamborine National Park - Another park which is a remainder of an extinct volcano, it is situated half way from the Gold Coast and Brisbane, it has many subtropical forests, waterfalls and animal life. The ascent is fairly steep, and may not be recommended for caravan trailers and heavy vehicle. At the top of the mountain, there is a small town (similar to a village) with a few rustic style restaurants, cafes, and shops, give that special touch to the mountain climate and atmosphere. Mt Tamborine is an amazing place with great views and the best sunsets on the coast. This place is simply a treasure not to be missed.

South e North Stradbroke Island - They are 2 islands with the North Island being the largest. Until not too long ago both island were one. A cyclone was responsible for dividing the island in two. Whales in northward migration can be observed close to the coast, especially from Point Lookout on North Stradbroke. Many desert beaches serve to all tastes, some with excellent Surf (although some with plenty of sharks too) and plenty of dolphins. The islands are great for camping, with many crystal clear freshwater lakes (In the North only) which are filtered by clean white sand. North Stradbroke has good basic infrastructure including, a few inns and hotels, restaurants, small markets and shops, camping and cabin for rent by the sea side and also 4x4 tours. It is definitely worth spending a day or weekend there. The Ferry boat for South Stradbroke Island, leaves Runaway Bay 7 days per week to the 10:30 of the morning. Extra boats function in other schedules and days of the week.

Muntjac, also known as Barking Deer, are small deer of the genus Muntiacus. Muntjac are the oldest known deer, appearing 15-35 million years ago, with remains found in Miocene deposits in France and Germany.

Description

The present-day species are native to South Asia and can be found from and Sri Lanka to southern China, Taiwan, Japan (Boso Peninsula and Oshima Island), India and

Indonesian islands. They are also found in the eastern Himalayas and in Burma. Inhabiting tropical regions, the deer have no seasonal rut and mating can take place at any time of year; this behaviour is retained by populations introduced to temperate countries.

Reeves's Muntjac has been introduced to England, with wild deer originating from escapes from Woburn Park around 1925. Muntjac have expanded very rapidly, and are now present in most English counties south of the M62 and have also expanded their range into Wales. The British Deer Society coordinated a survey of wild deer in the UK between 2005 and 2007 and reported that muntjac deer had noticeably expanded their range since the previous census in 2000. It is anticipated that muntjac may soon become the most numerous species of deer in England and may have also crossed the border into Scotland with a couple of specimens appearing in Northern Ireland in 2009; they have been spotted in the republic of Ireland in 2010, almost certainly having reached there with some human assistance.

Males have short antlers, which can regrow, but they tend to fight for territory with their "tusks" (downward-pointing canine teeth). The presence of these "tusks" is otherwise unknown in native British wild deer and can be discriminatory when trying to differentiate a Muntjac from an immature native deer, although Chinese Water Deer also have visible tusks (downward-pointing canine teeth); however, they are much less widespread.

Muntjac are of great interest in evolutionary studies because of their dramatic chromosome variations and the recent discovery of several new species. The Indian Muntjac is the mammal with the lowest recorded chromosome number: The male has a diploid number of 7, the female only 6 chromosomes. Reeves's muntjac (Muntiacus reevesi), in comparison, has a diploid number of 46 chromosomes.

The genus has 12 recognized species:

- Indian Muntjac or Common Muntjac, Muntiacus muntjak
- Reeves's Muntjac or Chinese Muntjac, Muntiacus reevesi
- Hairy-fronted Muntjac or Black Muntjac, Muntiacus crinifrons
- Fea's Muntjac, Muntiacus feae
- Bornean Yellow Muntjac, Muntiacus atherodes
- Roosevelt's Muntjac, Muntiacus rooseveltorum
- Gongshan Muntjac, Muntiacus gongshanensis
- Giant Muntjac, Muntiacus vuquangensis
- Truong Son Muntjac Muntiacus truongsonensis
- Leaf Muntjac Muntiacus putaoensis

Eco-Tourism in Andhra Pradesh

Andhra Pradesh is endowed with a rich and varied Bio-diversity distributed over a mosaic of different habitats spread over the Eastern Ghats, the Deccan Plateau Region, the Coastal Mangroves, the Fresh Water bodies like Kolleru and Brackish water bodies like the Pulicat and the grasslands of Rollapadu. These varied habitats have been supporting a variety of animal and plant species ranging from the Tiger, Gaur, Elephant, Black Buck and a variety of Deers and Antelopes, besides a variety of birds, including the Great Indian Bustard, the Spot bill Pelican, the Lesser Florican and the near extinct Jerdon's Courser. In addition to the above faunal species, the forests of Andhra Pradesh support about 5000 plant species consisting of species like Teak, Rosewood, Sandal Wood, and the endemic Red Sanders and Cycas beddomeii, etc.

Objectives of Eco-Tourism:

Eco-Tourism is "A responsible travel to natural areas, which conserves the environment and improves the welfare of the local people".

The primary objective of the Eco-Tourism is to show case the natural resource to different segments of the society, for viewing the nature and the natural processes for educational, recreational values and to propagate the message of environmental conservation.

To attract both domestic and foreign tourists by creating adequate infrastructure for accommodation, food and transport facilities in the Forest areas, Sanctuary areas and zoological gardens.

Activities

The main activities involved in Eco-Tourism are non-consumptive like Bird watching, Trekking, Nature trails, River rafting and more importantly mere watching of the scenic beauty of the Hills, Valleys, Meadows, Water bodies and the natural processes and learn to live in Nature. Eco-tourism also preaches the understanding and respecting various cultures and customs of people living in the area.

Role of A.P. Forest Development Corporation Ltd., in implementation of Eco-Tourism Project

The Government of AP has designated A.P. Forest Development Corporation Ltd., in G.O.Ms. No. 54 EFS&T (For.-II) Dept., Dt:26-6-2001, to implement the Eco-Tourism Projects in the Reserved Forests, Wildlife Sanctuaries, National Parks and Zoological Parks of the state.

The prime objective of these projects is to conserve the rich Biodiversity and propagate the message of environmental conservation to the people of Andhra Pradesh, by creating infrastructure facilities and visitor amenities by private participation.

In implementing the Eco-Tourism Projects the ownership of the land and all the assets created there on will remain with the Government of Andhra Pradesh, represented by APFDC, right from day one till the end of the Concession Agreement.

The private Developer will develop the Project as per the components approved by the Govt. with limited visitor amenities and maintain and operate the same till end of the concession period.

Some of the Eco-Tourism Projects being developed by APFDC are -

Sri Kotla Vijaya Bhaskar Reddy Botanical Garden:

Located in Kothaguda R.F. Block on Kondapur - Gachibowli Road near the Hi-tec City, Madapur, Hyderabad. The Botanical Gardens is being developed over an area of 128.07 Acres to conserve the plant Bio-diversity and to develop a Gene Bank apart from promoting the environmental education, botanical research and also to act as a recreation centre with a project outlay of about Rs.39 crores.

It is proposed to develop (18) Botanical Sectors exhibiting about 5000 species of plants collected through out sub-continent. Out of which, 7 sectors have been developed and opened to public viz., Rock Pool, Aquatic, Bamboo/ Canes, Palmarium/ Cycads, Tree grove, Ornamental and Medicinal Plants sectors. The balance sectors will be developed in the next three years through Private sector participation by the developer M/s. Delara Tourism Corporation Ltd.

Mahavir Nischalvan Eco-Tourism Centre:

Developed in Mahavir Harina Vanasthali National Parks, Vanasthalipuram, Hyderabad, a prominent Black Buck conservation area in the country spread over an area of 3605 Acres. The Park area comprises with wide variety of plant species and fauna like Black Buck, Cheetal, Wild Boar, Mongoose and different verities of birds. APFDC has developed an Eco-Tourism Centre at the Park with the following facilities for Cozy and Serene stay.

Mahavir Nischalvan Eco-Tourism Centre is situated 15 KMs from the city on Hyderabad - Vijayawada National Highway near Autonagar, Vanasthalipuram.

Tariff Details

AC Cottages	Rs.700/= per day
Non AC Tent Houses	Rs.400/- per day
10 Bedded Dormitory	Rs.100/- per day per bed
Amphitheatre	Rs.1000/- per day
Group Bookings available	

The following Eco-Tourism Projects are under process of implementation by the APFDC through private developers:

Sl. No.	Name of the Project	Outlay (Rs. In Crores)	Name of the Developer
1.	JLTC Shamirpet Deer Park, Shamirpet	1.20	M/s. Yasaswi Eco-Tourism, SPV of M/s, Shalivahana Project Ltd., Hyderabad.
2.	Night Safari and Eco Park at Kothaguda R.F.	70.00	M/s. TRAC India (P) Ltd.
3.	Bird Park at Kothaguda R.F.	32.70	M/s. Hyderabad Bird Park & Gardens Pvt. Ltd., Hyderabad.
4.	Mrugavani National Park, Chilkur	3.00	M/s. LJ Jungle Resorts & Eco-Tourism Pvt. Ltd., Hyderabad.

The Eco- Tourism Projects in Andhra Pradesh being implemented by APFDC Ltd., Hyderabad are operated on the principle of 'Design, Build, Finance, Operate and Maintain' (DBFO) Model with the participation of private Developers. The

Developer is given specific concession for the above purpose to operate in the Reserved Forest without any rights of ownership on the land or other assets created and are allowed to recoup his expenditure before the end of the concession period on profit sharing basis.

Ecotourism, ecotravel, ecolodges and just generally being "eco" have become popular tourism sales pitches. What is true ecotourism? What defines an ecolodge or an ecological company? How is the surrounding community involved? And finally, is ecotourism such a great thing anyways?

In order to truly understand ecotourism and all of it's attendant pros and cons it is necessary to do some background research. This page offers an introduction to the topic along with several links to more detailed information. The basic definitions below have been adapted and clarified from commonly used travel industry lingo. Some of the links are to articles that help further define ecotourism some promote it and some attack it but all are provocative and informative.

The goal of this page is neither to sell nor devalue ecotourism but rather to explore it as a concept and to help create informed travelers who ask lots of questions before, during and after their trip. Well informed travelers choose their guides, travel companies and lodges from a position of knowledge. This purchasing power can be the driving force behind positive or negative impacts on the places you visit.

There are almost as many terms to describe types of travel as there are travel companies. A couple of buzzwords that you often hear these days are "Eco-Tourism" and "Adventure Travel" . To further confuse the issue there is also "Sustainable Tourism", "Responsible Tourism", "Nature Based Travel", "Green Travel", "Multi-Sport Adventures" and "Cultural Tourism". The following are Untamed Path's definitions based on common usage.

Eco-tourism: Perhaps the most over-used and mis-used word in the travel industry. But what does it mean? The

Ecotourism Society defines it as "responsible travel to natural areas which conserves the environment and improves the welfare of the local people". A walk through the rainforest is not eco-tourism unless that particular walk somehow benefits that environment and the people who live there. A rafting trip is only eco-tourism if it raises awareness and funds to help protect the watershed. A loose interpretation of this definition allows many companies to promote themselves as something that they are not. If true eco-tourism is important to you, ask plenty of questions to determine if your trip will help "conserve and improve" the places you visit.

Adventure Travel: Another term which is heavily used by marketing departments. While travel to another country is often adventurous it is not necessarily "Adventure Travel". Most dictionaries define adventure similarly: "an unusual experience including some level of risk and uncertainty". "Adventure Travel" includes this idea of risk and oftentimes some unconventional means of transport. A dugout canoe journey deep into the Amazon basin with it's attendant difficulties meets this definition. While a city tour of Paris might have some level of uncertainty it is not by definition "Adventure Travel". If you love true adventure you probably already know this and can see through the hype to find the real thing for yourself.

There is sometimes a distinction made between "Soft" and "Hard" adventures. Soft adventures have a lower level of risk, greater comfort in accommodations and are less physically rigorous. Hard adventures often have very basic facilities, higher risk factor and greater physical challenge (ie: mountain climbing, backpacking or river expeditions).

Sustainable Tourism: Any form of tourism that does not reduce the availability of resources and does not inhibit future travelers from enjoying the same experience. If the presence of large numbers of tourists disturbs an animal's mating patterns so that there are fewer of that species in the future then that visit was not sustainable. Kayaking school on a free flowing river is an example of sustainable tourism. Big game hunting in Alaska is not.

Responsible Tourism: Tourism which operates in such a way as to minimize negative impacts on the environment. A wilderness camping trip using "Leave No Trace" ethics would be considered responsible tourism while dune buggy tours would not.

Nature-Based Tourism: A more generic term for any activity or travel experience with a focus on nature. Large jungle lodges fall into this category as do cruise ships to view penguins in Antarctica. These types of trips may or may not be environmentally sustainable or responsible. -

Green Tourism: Often used inter-changeably with eco-tourism and sustainable tourism but more accurately described as "any activity or facility operating in an environmentally friendly fashion". A lodge with composting toilets, gray water system, and solar powered lighting is probably "green". There are varying degrees of "greenness"; an awareness of where resources are coming from and where wastes are going is at the heart of the idea.

Multi-Sport Adventures: These trips have a focus on physical outdoor activities. Rafting, mountain biking, climbing, surfing, diving, etc. all offered in the same package. Not necessarily sustainable or eco but might be since many companies want to protect the areas where these activities take place.

Cultural Tourism: Interacting with and observing unique cultures is the focus of this style of trip. The concept of learning from other cultures to broaden ones perspective is usually a core value. An artisan showing you how to weave a tapestry and learning from them about their traditional dress would be a form of cultural tourism. Buying crafts in the market with no more interaction than the exchange of money does not provide the insight into another culture that is the central theme of cultural tourism.

Clearly all of these definitions are debatable. What one person or company calls "eco" another calls "sustainable" and so on. The main distinction between these terms is the motives and ethics behind them. Is the environment being cared for? Is there genuine effort to help the local economies? Are resources being left intact for future generations? Is the local culture being honored and valued and not just photographed? These questions will cut through the semantics and allow you to see what is really being offered.

At Untamed Path we've blended many of these ideas together to create our own unique form of travel. We place a high priority on preserving the places we visit, both environmentally and culturally. We enjoy active outdoor pursuits so many of our trips incorporate these sports but never at the expense of the natural world or the people who already live there. However, we don't make claims to be something that we can't live up to and are constantly reassessing our trips for ways to improve their ecological and cultural soundness. All of our trips contain elements of adventure travel, eco-tourism, multi-sport and cultural travel. We operate in a focused responsible and sustainable fashion and always, always have fun.

Chapter-2

Preparation While Going for Eco-tourism

The conscious attitude, actions, participation and interactions on the part of the individual traveler directly affect the outcome for all involved. As a thoughtful and responsible traveler there are several things you can do before, during and after your journey to ensure the experience is in line with the values of "ecotourism" and minimize your impact on the host country. It is far easier to simply go on vacation as an uninformed tourist but making the choice to be an informed traveler can have far reaching impacts on the world around us. The more you put into your trip the more you'll get out of it. The following is a code of conduct for responsible travelers.

1. Prepare for your trip: Educate yourself about your destination. Be on the lookout for news and current events about the area. Learn about local history, customs and culture as well as vital ecosystems. Learn at least the basics of the local language. A simple hello, please or thank you goes a long way. Approach travel with the desire to learn rather than just observe.

2. Respect local traditions and etiquette: Wear clothing that is accepted by the local culture. Be aware of people's sensitivity to being photographed; always ask first. Observe local customs. Be perceptive of your own cultural

values and how they affect your judgment of others. Remember that you are the visitor. There are many different concepts of time, personal space, communication etc. which are not wrong or inferior, just different. Act as an example for other travelers who are less informed than you.

3. Avoid ostentatious display of wealth: What may not seem a display of wealth to you may be considered extravagant by another culture. For example, a camera hanging around your neck or something as simple as a wristwatch or wedding band. Tuck these items away when visiting rural communities. Leave jewelry and other unnecessary valuables at home. They only create barriers and inhibit genuine interactions. Don't hand out sweets and loose change, this only serves to corrupt and create a begging mentality where none existed before.

4. Be flexible in your expectations: Approach your adventure with an open mind and you won't be disappointed. Sometimes plans change and an opportunity for more in-depth learning or a unique cultural experience presents itself. Adapt yourself to the situation rather than trying to adapt the situation to you.

5. Conserve resources: Often times the resources in an area visited by tourists are under a great deal of pressure already. Be aware of the resources that are being used because of your visit. This includes your personal consumption of items like water and wood for building fires or specialty foods that had to be transported from afar. Don't allow your guide to hunt endangered or threatened species or harvest rare plants for your consumption. A large luxury hotel in the middle of nowhere takes far more resources to build and maintain than does a small family run inn.

6. Practice environmental minimum impact: Follow the International Leave No Trace Rules. Pack out everything

that you bring in including toilet paper (if there is no toilet) or plastic water bottles (use purification tablets or a filter). Go to the bathroom at least 200 feet (70 paces) from any water source. Remove litter that others left behind. Do not remove any objects, plants or animal products from nature. Be aware of local endangered or threatened species so as not to purchase souvenirs made from their skin, feathers etc. Not only is this impactful on the environment but it is illegal.

7. Choosing a tour operator or guide: Thoroughly research your tour operator or guide by asking them pointed questions about specifically what they do that is "eco" and how they involve the local communities and economies. The "greening of tourism" has led companies to promote themselves as "eco" simply to sell trips. The larger the company with more luxurious accommodations, the less likely it is to be true ecotourism. Be persistent in your inquiries of an international or local tour operator.

8. Support local economies: How will your visit directly benefit the local economy or entire community? This is an integral part of true ecotourism. Use local transportation, guides, inns, restaurants and markets. This helps create a buffer zone for the environment surrounding protected natural areas by giving locals an economic alternative to potentially destructive practices. Community based ecotourism spreads the wealth and workload.

9. Bridging cultural gaps: Take the opportunity to be a cultural ambassador. Much of the world's image of western tourists is based on the unrealities of television and magazines. Look for situations for cultural exchange whereby learning about each other's lives is mutual. Getting to know the person sitting next to you on a local bus or the person cooking your food takes some effort but is often a rewarding experience.

10. Continued ecotourism: Ecotourism doesn't need to end with your flight home. Follow through on your commitment to conservation in your everyday life. Share your experiences with others to foster a greater understanding of our world. You will have seen and learned much from your journey. While it is still fresh in your heart and mind take action using the various agencies, grassroots organizations and resources available to you.

Conventional tourism is the kind of tourism which is connected to tracking of conventions, exhibitions etc. Conventional tourism represents an important market at an international level.

An important role to the growth of conventional tourism , is played by the availability of essential infrastructures and services, like amphitheatres, exhibition spaces, lodgings, infrastructures for coffee and dining, language translation services, etc. Also, the easy access to the place of realisation of a convention or an exhibition is a critical factor for the attracting of visitors.

Conventional tourism in the prefecture of Arta is being developed gradually during the last years. The required infrastructures for the realisation of conventions, like convention centres, suitable lodgings, road transport, etc are available. Especially at the town of Arta the amphitheatrical hall of DIONI that belongs to the Municipality of Arta is found, the SKOYFAS hall that belongs the music club "SKOYFAS" as well as the halls of the hotels ARTA PALACE and BYZANTINO near the town of Arta. Consequently, the potential of convention realisation exists.

The geographic positioning of the Prefecture, a nodal point in North-western Greece, the natural wealth, the protected from the treaty of RAMSAR, NATURA 2000 etc locations, the rich historical - ecclesiastical and cultural heritage of the region, but also the seat of Technological Educational Institute of Epirus in the town of Arta, help Arta's prospect for the realisation of scientific conventions, offering at the same time high conventional services, and also recreation.

Adventure Travel & Non-conventional Tourism in Peru

Apumayo Expediciones, a local Peruvian company based in the City of Cusco, established in 1995. Specialized in adventure travel and non conventional tourism, combining it with cultural, educational and natural history. Apumayo Expediciones describes itself as a commercial venture with a strong environmental and social agenda, development and supporting in the way many projects like river clean up`s, offering activities and tours for people with disabilities and support Andean community projects, which maximise the positive effect of tourism activities locally. The Community of Cachiccata near Ollantaytambo and Machu Picchu, host many of our adventure trips like rafting, hiking, mountain bike, horse back rides and other participative activities related with the Inca culture and the day life of the Andean people like agro-tourism, interpretation, volunteer and bring the option to share authentic experiences with the local inhabitants.

Classical Cusco 5 Days / 4 Nights

Code: CC-7Cf/09

Grading: Easy - No need experience

Duration: 5 Days / 4 Nights.

Season: April to October

Departures: Private and group service any moment

Itinerary

Day 01: Cusco - City Tour

Transfer form the airport to the hotel. Morning to acclimatize. After lunch in a restaurant of your choice we will meet for a city tour. This tour includes a visit to the Cathedral which is over 450 years old and the magnificent ruins of Sacsayhuaman, Kenko and Tambomachay.

At night we will have the opportunity to dinner together in one of Cusco's finest restaurants.

Day 02: Sacred Valley

Following a delicious breakfast at your hotel you will be met by your guide who will take you on a tour of The Sacred Valley of the Incas. This tour includes the fantastic Inca complex of Pisac a look round the local market a buffet lunch and tour of the village and fortress of Ollantaytambo returning to Cusco in the evening. The night is free for you to eat in a restaurant of your choice; although we always have plenty of suggestions for you should you require them.

Day 03: Machu Picchu

For most of you this is the main reason that you are here. To fulfill that childhood dream of visiting the citadel of Machu Picchu. We will take the Vistadomme class train which allows spectacular views on the road to Machu Picchu. A private tour of Machu Picchu where we will receive explanations on the history of Machu Picchu. Return train to Cusco and free evening.

Day 04: Free Day Cusco

Free Day to, allow you to do some shopping and explore some of the other places of interest in Cusco. At night we will have a farewell dinner with a typical dancing show.

Day 05: Transfer Out

Breakfast and transfer to Cusco airport for your flight to Lima. End of our services.

Apumayo Expediciones is situated in Cusco, the gateway city to the Inca empire and Machu Picchu. We also operate all over Peru and able to customize any kind of activity such multi-city programs, logistics for expeditions, film or research crews and multi-activities itineraries. They specialise in the city historical attractions and its surroundings and all areas of Peru, including the Amazon jungle and the desert coast.

In the past, Apumayo Expediciones open some new adventure destinations for kayaking and rafting like the Colca and Cotahuasi rivers where we did the first explorations and commercial journeys. In the present we are open new alternatives for hiking and trekking supporting by Llamas, following lost Inca trails near Machu Picchu and running a new and spectacular section of the Apurimac river call "the black canyon" which is the source of the Amazon river.

Denver is an expanding metropolis that manages to retain a compact feel, thanks to its increasingly hips neighborhoods with names like LoDo (Lower Downtown) and LoHi (Lower Highlands). Getting around on foot or public transportation is easy, and the buses that run along the 16th Street Mall (a pedestrian shopping strip) are free. o Although some people view Denver mostly as a jumping off point for skiing, hiking and biking in Red Rocks Park and the mountains, the truth is there's plenty to do indoors, and out, right in the city. When the politicians, delegates and media clear out after the Democratic National Convention that begins Monday, the city will be all yours. Here are 10 possibilities for what to do and see:

Denver Art Museum

Daniel Libeskind designed the dramatic, titanium-clad Frederic C. Hamilton Building, which opened in 2006 and connects to Gio Ponti's 1971 North Building via a glassed-in second-floor bridge with good views of what's called the "Golden Triangle Museum District." More than 50,000 square feet of new gallery space - with nary a straight wall and plenty of mazelike layouts - showcase modern and contemporary, Oceanic, and Western American art, as well as temporary exhibits, among them "Landscapes from the Age of Impressionism" (through Sept. 7) and "Clyfford Still Unveiled" (through Nov. 16), an informal preview for the museum dedicated to the early abstract impressionist that's opening next door in 2010. Head to the older building for everything from American Indian art to the design and textile collections.

Museum of Contemporary Art

Opened with great fanfare in October, this striking glass box designed by architect David Adjaye deserves kudos for taking advantage of natural light. Exhibits in galleries devoted to such disciplines as photography and new media are temporary. August attractions include Jane Hammond's photos (opened Aug. 19) and a 24-hour outdoor sculpture installation by Nora Ligorano and Marshall Reese starting at noon Tuesday titled "The State of Things."

Best bet: Hang out at the MCA's rooftop cafe and enjoy the garden and people-watching.

Colorado State Capitol

The white granite, gold leaf-domed Colorado State Capitol designed by Elijah E. Myers and built in the 1890s with mostly local materials (including lots of gorgeous rose marble) is worth seeing, whether you take a free 45-minute tour or wander around by yourself. Don't miss Denverite Alan True's murals depicting Colorado water use (with commentary written in 1940 by Colorado poet laureate Thomas Hornsby Ferrill) surrounding the grand staircase; bronze elevator doors chronicling the state's history with bison, teepees and other symbols; stained-glass windows; and the council chambers. Make an appointment to visit the dome for panoramic views of the Rocky Mountains. A tip: Stand on the 13th step on the west side of the building, and you're exactly 1 mile above sea level.

Kirkland Museum of Fine and Decorative Art

Denver's quirkiest museum feels more like a classy antique shop, thanks to the organized jumble of decorative arts, regional art (with an emphasis on Colorado Modernism) and Vance Kirkland paintings. Kirkland used the original 1910-11 arts and crafts building as his art school/studio, surrounding himself with works by his contemporaries, as well as art nouveau, art deco and other beautifully designed objects. His heir, Hugh Grant, kept adding to the furniture, ceramics, glassware, etc., eventually expanding the building and opening to the public in 2003. Be sure to check out the charming sculpture garden.

Afterward walk up the street to Liks Ice Cream Parlor for creamy house-made ice creams in myriad flavors, quite a few of them invented by customers.

Big Blue Bear

More than 300 public artworks dot the city, and part of the fun is coming upon them by surprise. One of my favorites - and everybody's, I suspect - is the 40-foot-high, vibrant blue bear peeking in the windows of the Colorado Convention Center. Its real title is I See What You Mean, and artist Lawrence Argent created it in 2005 out of steel encased in a cement/fiberglass composite. He has called it his "stylized representation of native fauna."

Larimer Square

Saved from destruction in the 1960s and renovated as the first urban renewal project of its kind, Denver's oldest block is lined with Victorian brick buildings housing trendy stores, restaurants and night spots. Shop for Western- and Asian-influenced clothing, collectibles and home accessories at Cry Baby Ranch; designer duds and gifts for infants and kids (up to age 8) at Cute as a Button; and women's fashions and accessories at several boutiques. Then stop in at Corridor 44, the city's first Champagne bar, for a glass of bubbly before savoring plump mussels with frites and other French classics at Bistro Vendome or fresh bacon with curry-scented chickpea puree, grilled Colorado lamb with braised organic greens and a bevy of Mediterranean-influenced creations at Rioja.

Rockmount Ranch Wear

No enterprise epitomizes Denver's pioneer spirit more than Rockmount, started in 1946 and known for making the first Western shirts with snaps. Worn in dozens of films by stars ranging from Elvis Presley to Meg Ryan, the signature "diamond" snap, "sawtooth" pocket designs in more than 100 fabrics fill the racks on the spacious first floor of the five-story, 1908 brick building, complemented by skirts, boots, hats, belts and everything else a cowboy or girl needs. Most amazing is that founder Jack A. "Papa" Weil, who also was the first to produce bolo ties commercially, came to work every weekday morning until his death earlier this month at age 107.

Highlands

Walk or bike across Millennium Bridge, one of three pedestrian bridges (you'll know it by the ship's mast public sculpture) from the Riverfront area. That will put you in LoHi, the newly hip gateway to the Highlands, Denver's largest neighborhood, just northwest of downtown. Highlands Square and the Tennyson Street Cultural District (at 10, the city's oldest art district) are the neighborhood's other main commercial strips, and the many family-owned ethnic restaurants reflect waves of immigrants, especially Hispanic and Italian. Nowadays, loft developments are sprinkled among the bungalows. Three parks, all with lakes, include Sloan's Park with motor boats and jet skis, and Berkeley Park across the street from the old-fashioned Lakeside Amusement Park, which, along with its carousel, turns 100 this year.

Dazzle Restaurant and Lounge

Denver has plenty of great places to hear live music, but Dazzle (930 Lincoln St.) stands out because the comfortable setting appeals to such a wide audience. Local, national and international jazz artists perform seven nights a week in both the lounge and the restaurant. The menu goes beyond bar food, brunch is a big favorite and the happy hour is one of the best in town with $4 premium drinks and $5 small plates. No wonder a dazzled Downbeat magazine dubbed it one of the 100 best clubs in the world.

Denver Performing Arts Complex

Ten venues make up the country's second largest performing arts complex, so on any given night you can see Broadway musicals on tour, Tony Award-winning shows, offbeat theater, opera, the symphony and maybe a ballet after entering through the blocklong, 80-foot-high glass atrium. The Ellie Caulkins Opera House, which opened in 2005 as the state-of-the-art home of Opera Colorado, is in the building that originally was the multipurpose Municipal Auditorium, where the 1908 Democratic National Convention took place. Hot chef Kevin Taylor has a restaurant in the basement.

Indians believe in holidays: The country has among the largest number of public holidays in the world. Yet the most common reason for getting away is to "visit a native place." Migrant workers return to their family farms at harvest time. Others return to their villages (and extended families) for an annual pilgrimage. The concept of a holiday where you let your hair down and relax has been accepted only in recent years.

The idea of rural tourism is, therefore, a bit of a puzzle for many Indians. They go back to their village every year; why should they pay good money to go to some other village? Rustic charms hold greater appeal for foreign tourists. Concerted government and travel industry efforts to sell India abroad with campaigns such as "Incredible India" began only this decade, but rural tourism as a product is still evolving.

A national tourism policy was introduced in 2002, with rural tourism identified as a focus area to generate employment and promote sustainable livelihoods. "As a part of the National Tourism Policy 2002, the Ministry of Tourism is developing and promoting rural tourism sites which have core competency in art, craft, culture, heritage, handloom, etc.," Union Ministry of Tourism Secretary Sujit Banerjee said recently in a statement. According to the 2002 policy, "Special thrust should be imparted to rural tourism and tourism in small settlements, where sizable assets of our culture and natural wealth exist."

Just what is rural tourism? The government has taken a broad view. "Any form of tourism that showcases rural life, art, culture and heritage at rural locations, thereby benefiting the local community economically and socially as well as enabling interaction between the tourists and the locals for a more enriching tourism experience, can be termed as rural tourism," says a Ministry of Tourism policy paper. "Rural tourism is essentially an activity which takes place in the countryside. It is multifaceted and may entail farm/agricultural tourism, cultural tourism, nature tourism, adventure tourism and ecotourism. As against conventional tourism, rural tourism has certain typical characteristics: It is experience-oriented; the locations are sparsely populated; it is predominantly in natural environments; it meshes with seasonality and local events; and it is based on the preservation of culture, heritage and traditions."

Not everyone applies such a broad definition. Ecotourism which concerns itself with the preservation of the environment while offering the best to tourists -- is more fashionable these days. And some in government and the tourism industry would like to focus on ecotourism rather than rural tourism, which could have a down-market, rough-it-out connotation. "Ecotourism and rural tourism are not exactly the same but can be clubbed together for greater benefits," says Md. Jawaid, a former minister in the eastern state of Bihar who has promoted the website ecotourismindia.com. "This is just an information site now," Jawaid says. "It is a small effort on my part to promote tourism in the rural areas of India. But we have big plans. The potential is huge."

Rajesh K. Aithal, assistant professor of marketing at the Indian Institute of Management, Lucknow, has another definition. "Rural tourism is a form of tourism in which the guests get to enjoy the unique culture of village life through participation in events, or experiencing the local cuisine, or buying ethnic goods, and in the process also improve the welfare of the local people."

Two Types of Tourism

Mandip Singh Soin, president of the Ecotourism Society of India, a group of tourism professionals and environmentalists formed with the Ministry of Tourism's backing, says the concept can be confusing. "Rural tourism is understood differently in different parts of the world," he notes. "Ecotourism and rural tourism are the same only in a sense. They are cousins really. Rural tourism may not necessarily be the protector and enhancer of conservation. It is much more community-oriented. Ecotourism is more holistic; all responsible tourism actions come into play."

The difference is best illuminated by a couple of examples. As part of its 2002 plan, the government partnered with the United Nations Development Program (UNDP) for an Endogenous Tourism Project. Some 30 rural sites were selected in 20 states to develop as destinations for rural tourists. The UNDP pumped in an initial US$2.5 million. The government asked the states and union territories to submit proposals. Those that were selected were entitled to assistance up to US$100,000.

One of the project's success stories is Hodka village in Gujarat. A village tourism committee owns and operates the Shaam-e-Sarhad ("Sunset at the Border") Village Resort. The accommodations are simple. Tourists can stay in tents or traditional mud huts, known as bhungas. All have attached bathrooms, Western toilets and showers. The resort can accommodate up to 30 people. Staying in tents costs around US$40 a night, while the bhungas are more expensive, around US$60 a night. Among the attractions: specially organized workshops in embroidery and leather work; interactions with other artisan communities; wildlife including flamingos, pelicans, foxes and leopards; and nearby archaeological sites of the Indus Valley Civilization. In January 2008, there was even a pashu mela -- a cattle fair. All this activity has had to be organized, packaged and sold.

Far away from Hodka, in the northeastern state of Meghalaya, is Mawlynnong. Neither the UNDP nor the government of India has been involved with this ecotourism effort's success. Rather, a community effort has made it the poster child of rural tourism in India. In 2003, Discover India (a magazine published by Media Transasia along with the Union Ministry of Tourism) anointed it the cleanest village in Asia. It has retained its charms. "Mawlynnong's reputation for cleanliness has even earned it a place on the state's tourism map," according to a report by the BBC. "Hundreds of visitors from all over India now visit the village throughout the year." Mawlynnong also attracts tourists from around the world.

Both Mawlynnong and Hodka demonstrate a key prerequisite for the success of any rural tourism project: community involvement. "Going by our experience in setting up community-owned companies in the rural sector, the outcome depends on a number of factors, and host communities should be encouraged to play a pivotal role in the development of rural tourism," says William Bissell, managing director of Fabindia and author of the recently published Making India Work. Fabindia is a novel experiment in which rural artisans --

the suppliers to this private retail platform -- are shareholders in the company.

Community Involvement

The point about community involvement is also made by Mott MacDonald, a global management, engineering and development consultancy that the Ministry of Tourism asked to evaluate the rural tourism scheme. Its report, submitted in June 2007 after five years of operation, says: "In order to make the scheme more meaningful, it is very important that the sustenance issues be discussed with the community before the start of the project." Fear of the unknown once was common, but it has disappeared in the projects undertaken. "Xenophobia has been removed from the minds of the local people," the report notes.

Before the Ministry of Tourism became involved, this fear of foreigners was just one of the basic issues that hindered the flow of tourists to the sites chosen by the government and the UNDP. From the start, the sites had the advantages of historical importance, craft, culture, cuisine and natural beauty. But hindrances included a lack of basic infrastructure including sanitation, drinking water and wayside amenities; a lack of accommodation and food facilities; and a lack of awareness about site importance and the need for local guides.

Most of the issues have been addressed. "With the intervention of the Ministry of Tourism, there has been considerable change," the Mott MacDonald report notes. "The rural tourism scheme has been a valuable vehicle to bring the ultimate rural stakeholders in touch with the tourism sector to increase employment." The report continues: "Rural tourism is not the end, but the means to stimulate economic growth, to increase the viability of underdeveloped locations, and to improve the living standards of local populations." Adds Bissell of Fabindia: "With proper training and the infrastructure in place, rural tourism certainly has the potential to generate large-scale employment. What we need is commitment and a long-term view."

"The development of a strong platform around the concept of rural tourism is definitely useful for a country like India, where almost 74% of the population resides in its seven million villages," the Ministry of Tourism's policy paper notes.

A Nod to the Bottom Line

Yet increasing the bottom line for tourism is equally important. After all, there is a limit to the number of tourists you can pack into the Taj Mahal and Khajuraho. Today, with exports plummeting amid the global economic slowdown, tourism has become a key foreign-exchange earner. According to Ministry of Tourism figures, foreign-exchange earnings from tourism in 2008 were around US$11 billion, an increase of 14.4% from 2007. A total of 5.37 million tourists visited India in 2008, an increase of 5.6% from 2007. But in the first nine months of 2009, foreign tourist arrivals were down 7.7% from the same period a year earlier. Earnings will also be down, though those numbers are not yet available.

The government is doing all it can to boost these figures. In October, at a Dubai road show for its Visit India 2009 tourism campaign, Pronab Sarkar, secretary of the Indian Association of Tour Operators (IATO), unveiled some highlights for foreign tourists. Among them: an IATO-sponsored complimentary one-day rural eco-holiday in the country.

Tour operators are businessmen. Would they be bothered about the larger picture of rural employment and sustainability? Yes, says Soin of the Ecotourism Society. The society was set up last year because "we feel we needed to have our tourism sector do the right thing in terms of responsible tourism actions that would allow for a smaller tourism footprint ecologically. At the same time, we wanted to look at how tourism can get its dollars to flow down the supply chain more equitably and involve the local communities to be partners in tourism operations. We also want to be the watchdog of tourism in the country."

Soin responds to criticism that rural tourism exploits poor people in the villages and damages the environment. "This is not correct," he says. "Most revenues are being earned and kept at the village level so it goes into the pockets of the villagers either as direct individual earnings or collective cooperative efforts. In fact, in areas like [the northeastern state of] Nagaland, where the ecology was being damaged by village lads hunting rare pheasants, the trend got reversed when they saw the opportunity for earning money as guides showing these pheasants to bird watchers." Adds Aithal of IIM: "A well-executed rural tourism project has the potential of becoming a win-win proposition both for the tourist and the villagers."

There is a lot of potential for rural tourism in India, Aithal notes. "'Rural' as an entity is fast disappearing, especially in the developed world. Even for young urban Indians, rural would be something that they would want to connect to." Adds Jawaid of ecotourismindia.com: "Both Indians and foreigners can be targeted." For the moment, however, it's the foreign tourist who is being wooed. "Initially, the target will be foreigners as this is a novelty for them," Soin says. "It may not be that novel an experience for Indians. Indians demand more comfort in lodging and are less prone to roughing it out."

"Rural tourism is in its nascent stage in India," Aithal notes. "But it will grow. There is a huge market out there. The experience of many countries shows that rural tourism can be seen as an alternate source of livelihood and employment. The main problems with rural tourism are the same as with any rural development project. Can you scale up these projects? Can you replicate them? And how do you make these projects stand on their own without money being pumped in from outside? For this you need very strong village-level institutions, which can take up the execution once the project has been initiated."

According to Fabindia's Bissell, "If sites are selected with care, on the basis of potential and core competency, and the project implementation focuses as much on the 'software' aspects of human development along with the 'hardware' of capacity building and infrastructure development, there is every reason to anticipate a positive outcome. As a multi-sectoral activity, using multiple services provided by a range of suppliers, rural tourism is an area where a strong public-private partnership is of prime importance, particularly given the number of ministries beyond tourism -- for example, rural development, culture, environment and tribal welfare -- that could be involved."

Kanyakumari is the land's end of Indian mainland. It is one of holiest Punya Theerthams of Hindus. It is here Swami Vivekanada meditated and had the vision of India's future glory. A magnificent rock memorial adores the rock where he meditated. There is also the famous Thiruvalluvar statue. Then there is the famous Kanyakumari Amman temple. Virgin Goddess meditates in the south just as how Siva meditates in the northern Himalayan mountain ranges thus symbolising the spiritual unity of India. Kanyakumari is part of Kanyakumari district. This district contains many interesting and mysterious traditional dimensions unknown to pilgrims and tourists who visit Kanyakumari.

However be warned that this is not for every one. Only those with the thirst for knwoledge and who seek truth can find them. Once found these features are enchanting.

PREPARING FOR YOUR ECOTOURISM TRIP

Ecotourism Training

It is one thing to see rare wildlife in their native habitat, but to actually understand how rare these brilliant creatures are and fully comprehend their behavior in certain situations is another. Read books such as naturalists' memoirs and wildlife guides are a good place to start. Try to feel what the experts do when they explore the rainforest. Be prepared to distinguish the subtle differences of species apart. Try to memorize charts of different plant and animal species in the destination you intend to explore, and then take the charts with you when you travel. Native literature is important as well to help understand the relationship the local people and tribes have with plants and animals.

Attending lectures by scientists and experts at colleges, universities, libraries, and local clubs is also a good way to learn a bit more about what is going on. Take a visit your local zoo or botanical garden as well. Chances are they will have at least some of the flora and fauna you will be seeing when you take your trip.

A good general fitness level is important to be an ecotourist. While many tours are simply just sitting on a boat, the majority involves a great deal of walking. This includes everything from hiking on volcanic beaches, following trails through the jungle or the steep hills of a cloud forest, slogging through thick mud, and light walking along gravel paths beside your resort or lodge. If hiking to isolated areas, you may need to be in great shape. You may be hiking up and down mountains, in extreme heat, and carrying a large load of food and equipment.

Ecotourism Gear

There is no piece of equipment that is absolutely necessary to be an ecotourist. The most memorable encounter you will have when looking for wildlife is that time that the animal happened to be sitting in the tree above you or crossed the path in front of you. There are a number of accessories that will make your trip easier and allow you to make the most of where you are.

Binoculars are an easy tool that can give you a much better view of a bird or an animal. Considering you rarely can get too close to wildlife, binoculars will allow you to see the creatures while they are hundreds of meters away or hidden amongst the dense foliage of the rainforest. Similarly, zoom lenses on cameras will improve your photos significantly when shooting wildlife that is often very small or far away. Go for lenses no smaller than 200mm. Lenses that are 300mm, 400mm, or higher are recommended for shooting birds. Your point and shoot, even with a small zoom, can get you some decent shots too when animals are extremely close, but don't expect national geographic type shots.

Wildlife/birding guides for identifying different species can be a great help. Mosquito repellents are a must. A flashlight for hikes in the night and walking around the lodge or campground is a good item to have. Long sleeved clothing, even better if waterproof, are good for protecting against the sun and creepy crawlies.

ATEC-Promoting Sustainable Travel

ATEC is Puerto Viejo's original eco-tourism provider. We work to help visitors find fun ecologically and socially responsible activities to entertain themselves while in Talamanca, Limon, Costa Rica.

Founded back in 1989, ATEC funded the training a group of about 20 guides. Now from this website and our little office in Puerto Viejo, we represent over 100 fabulous local guides. We encourage you to support ATEC and participate in local, sustainable travel in Talamanca!

ATEC is a self-sustaining non-profit association that supports itself, its guides, and its efforts through your support. THANK YOU!

You came to Costa Rica to get to know Costa Rica, do it with Costa Ricans!

At ATEC we promote culturally and ecologically sound tourism and small-scale, locally owned and responsible businesses. We stimulate conservation through education and by helping local associations and families derive economic benefits from their natural resources.

Our Goals

- Promote the development of an ecological and socially responsible tourism in Talamanca
- Promote ethnic pride and cultural expression among the indigenous and Afro-Caribbean residents
- Promote the initiation and management of locally owned businesses and tourist services.
- To fulfill ATEC's goals our office, located in Old Harbour (Puerto Viejo), serves as a communication center to put visitors in contact with experienced native naturalist guides who offer a variety of interesting, educational field experiences. These guided hikes are by appointment and, under normal circumstances, limited to 6 persons.

As the world gets wise to the positive impact of green travel and ecotourism, more and more people want to contribute.

"What better way to do so than with an ecotourism volunteers vacation?

Volunteer vacations are an excellent way to learn more about green travel and ecotourism while giving back. Besides, we've all been on the lay-by-the-pool vacation and giving back is so much more rewarding! There are literally hundreds of opportunities to go on a vacation and give back to a local community or environment. Volunteer vacations, while a relatively new phenomenon are popping up all over the planet, offering people the opportunity to travel, see a new place and give back.

Having a volunteer abroad vacation can mean traveling to Latin America to help local communities with sustainable agriculture, visiting Australia's coastlines to help clean, working in your own community with Habitat For Humanity, working with the Himalayan Light Foundation, contributing to the Sierra Club or working with marine life to make eroding coastal regions last. There are even volunteer vacations for families and seniors!

Volunteer vacations can last a few days, but are typically structured to last two weeks or more. Because these organizations need focused help at certain times of the year, many of them require that you apply months before hand in order to be approved for the vacation. Some of the work can be fairly labor intensive as well, so making sure that you are signed up for a volunteer vacation that fits your physical abilities is important not only for your health but for the organizations you will be working under.

Join short-term volunteers in our non-profit network providing long-term, ethical service on a volunteer vacation abroad or a USA volunteer program. Live and work with local people on life-affirming service programs for one to three weeks. Extended-term service option for six to 24 weeks.

We need you here now: Care for babies in Romania or lend your helping hands and giving heart to the Blackfeet Nation in Montana! 50% of our volunteers return on another service program!

"I have great respect for Global Volunteers' philosophy and policies. With each trip, I'm touched and humbled by the possibility of helping a child or young adult. Global Volunteers enables me to not just be a passive world traveler but to be an active participant, a "citizen diplomat." Norina Vaira, volunteer on 18 teams

"Global Volunteers has, without a doubt, the best programs in the field." - TravelSmart Newsletter Mobilizing over 27,000 volunteers on six continents since 1984, we're a long-standing NGO leader in Special Consultative Status with the United Nations and UNICEF. We support some 100 service partnerships year around through short-term volunteer teams, direct project funding, classroom support, child sponsorships and student scholarships. Join our programs serving local people as a family, group or individual. No specialized skills are needed to contribute genuine, long-term development assistance.

"We recommend Global Volunteers."

- Travel and Leisure Magazine

"A model that has been replicated worldwide."

- San Francisco Chronicle

Richard Denman is Director of The Tourism Company, a UK based tourism consultancy. Following a masters degree from Cambridge University and a doctorate from the University of Edinburgh, he worked at a senior level with the tourist boards in England before setting up The Tourism Company on 1990. Richard is a leading international expert on ecotourism and the sustainable development of tourism destinations. He produced WWF's Guidelines on Community Based Ecotourism. He has worked closely with the UN World Tourism Organization and UNEP, initially as consultant for the World Summit on Ecotourism and subsequently in preparing a number of documents for them on sustainable tourism, including the policy guide Making Tourism More Sustainable. Other areas of work with UNWTO include poverty alleviation through tourism and stakeholder partnership models. Within Europe, he has coordinated the work of the European Union's Tourism Sustainability Group and helped to set up the European Charter for Sustainable Tourism in Protected Areas. He has recently been working as a consultant to the Tourism Sustainability Council, advising on a global accreditation programme for certification schemes.

Richard has worked on national and local projects in over 25 countries, including tourism plans, feasibility studies, product development and policy guidance. He is a former Board Director of The International Ecotourism Society, a member of Europe's ECOTRANS network.

Ecotourism

Ecotourism International has supported ecolodge development projects and ecotourism planning initiatives in North, Central and South America, Africa, Asia, and the Middle East. The company's core competence is in preparing market assessments, feasibility studies, business plans, investment proposals, and policy analyses for ecotourism and sustainable tourism projects.

Ed Sanders, President of Ecotourism International, is a frequent speaker on the business aspects of ecolodge development and operations. He is a former Vice-Chairman of the Board of The International Ecotourism Society (TIES) and a founding director of Sustainable Travel International. He is author of The Business of Ecolodges: A Survey of Ecolodge Economics and Finance (TIES, 2001) and the U.S. Ecotourism Market (World Tourism Organization, 2002). He is a founding partner in a world-class, 13,000 acre (20-square mile) conservation and ecotourism project in southern Belize. This for-profit ecotourism venture anchors a much larger public/private/non-profit habitat corridor that protects the last remaining stretch of tropical forest connecting the mountains to the coast of Belize.

In order to complement his business planning services, Ed Sanders collaborates with some of the country's leading ecotourism experts and specialized companies, including:

- Natural resource and recreation master planners
- Interpretive specialists
- Ecolodge and landscape architects
- Environmental engineers
- Interior designers
- Green building and energy efficiency specialists
- Ecotourism generalists
- Tourism marketing experts

- Community development planners

Ecotourism in Afghanistan

Tourism in Afghanistan? It's not what you expect from this remote and beautiful, but troubled Central Asian nation. Most media reports on Afghanistan talk of war and bloodshed, insurgents and explosive devices. What they rarely report is that most of the northern half of the country is in fact quite peaceful and that reconstruction and development are moving forward.

A trickle of adventurous tourists is already arriving in Afghanistan, reminding Afghans of the heady days of the 1960s and 1970s when their country was a popular destination for thousands of foreign visitors, and tourism was good business. Those who came then ranged from archaeologists and ethnographers to hippies and other Western youth looking for adventure in high Asia.

The Aga Khan Development Network (AKDN), one of the world's largest private development agencies, works extensively in South and Central Asia. In two regions of Afghanistan (and in neighbouring Tajikistan), the Network is now supporting cautious plans to help revive the tourist industry as a way of creating jobs, and also to ensure that the inevitable tourism developments remain under the control of local people.

AKDN has ecotourism programmes in two areas - the remote and mysterious Wakhan Corridor, in the panhandle of northeastern Afghanistan, sandwiched between Pakistan, China and Tajikistan; and in the serenely beautiful Bamyan region of central Afghanistan, site of the giant Buddha statues destroyed by the Taleban.

The first concern is, of course, security. Both the Wakhan and Bamyan are generally safe and peaceful. Wakhan is so remote it was virtually untouched by the years of war. Bamyan, high in the Central Highlands, has always been somewhat removed from the mainstream of Afghan politics and has been quiet since the end of the Taleban regime in 2001. These ecotourism programmes are aimed at long-term development, helping local people to prepare for a tourism industry which is already reviving.

Afghanistan is not for the fainthearted traveller, but several thousand expatriates already live and work here. Most are accustomed to the country's special circumstances and could provide a ready market for the sort of small-scale trekking and adventure tourism which both Wakhan and Bamyan can provide. Apart from foreign tourists, Bamyan is already a popular destination for Afghans who visit the area in large numbers in summer. The ecotourism programme is also aimed at this market, to attract more Afghan visitors and to help them better understand the region's local culture and ecology.

Of the two regions, Bamyan is better known internationally because the valley was the site of two giant Buddha statues carved into the red cliffs, dating from the 6th century. These were famously destroyed in 2001 by the Taleban. The giant niches where the Buddhas were carved remain, as well as hundreds of caves dug into the cliffs by Buddhist monks in the 1st millennium AD.

Bamyan was then a key transit point through the Hindu Kush mountains for travellers on the Silk Road trade routes which linked China, Europe and India. The Bamyan valley is also rich in other archaeological and historical sites, all set in a sublime landscape of green fields, ochre cliffs, cave complexes and fantastic wind-eroded rock formations reminiscent of Cappadocia in Turkey.

Another well-known site in the Bamyan region is Band-e-Amir, a chain of seven turquoise lakes formed by natural dams which have just become the centrepiece of Afghanistan's first national park, declared in May 2009. Also nearby is the Ajar Valley, a spectacular secluded valley which was once the private hunting preserve of Afghanistan's last king.

The Bamyan Ecotourism Programme, funded by the government of New Zealand, and implemented by AKDN, got underway this year. A tourist information office has been established in Bamyan, and brochures, a website and other information materials are being prepared. Local guides are being trained in the history, geology and folklore of the area.

Training is also getting underway to help establish small private guesthouses, and training courses will upgrade the quality of services at local hotels and restaurants. At Band-e-Amir, campsites will be developed, and local people helped to set up horse trekking and other tourist services.

The programme will stress the preservation and development of local culture and the protection of the natural environment as assets which are essential for a profitable tourism industry. In remote, poor areas with few natural resources like Bamyan and Wakhan, such assets as natural beauty and a vibrant indigenous culture can be exploited to attract visitors and money to develop the local economy.

The Wakhan Corridor is very different from Bamyan, culturally, ethnically and geographically, but this great valley of the upper Amu Darya, or Oxus, river was also an important part of the Silk Road since it was one of the chief routes through the mountain ranges of Central Asia on the way to China. Marco Polo became the Wakhan's most famous early tourist when he travelled along the valley in about 1270. The Wakhan was also a focus of the "Great Game" in the late 19th century when rival British and Russian explorers and spies came to find the source of the Oxus, or to win imperial influence in this little-known region.

The Wakhan Corridor and the Afghan Pamirs is an area tailor-made for the adventurous traveller keen to trek with a horse or a yak through unknown valleys and camp in yurts in the high summer pastures of the last Kyrgyz nomads. A network of small family-run guesthouses has been established along the length of the Wakhan valley which visitors can now use as a base for exploring the region, whether by vehicle, or (preferably) by horse or on foot. Information brochures are being prepared and a website will be ready soon, giving detailed information. Training courses here will also help to improve the standard of food and accommodation, which at present are very basic.

Wakhan also has some of the highest mountains of the Hindu Kush - Mt Noshaq, at 7492 metres, is Afghanistan's highest peak. Wakhan was emerging as a new mountaineering destination in the 1960s and 70s, until the Soviet invasion of 1979. With the recent publication of a mountaineering guidebook for Wakhan, steps are now underway to develop the region's mountaineering potential. In a notable achievement, two local Afghan mountain guides, trained as part of the ecotourism programme, recently became the first Afghans ever to stand on top of their country's highest mountain, when they climbed to the summit of Mt Noshaq on 19 July this year.

For visitors coming to Afghanistan from outside the country, some are uneasy about travelling through the capital, Kabul, where there have been well-publicised bombings. Fortunately, there is another option for getting to Wakhan - a recently opened border crossing into Afghanistan from the Gorno-Badakhshan region of neighbouring Tajikistan at Ishkashim, the gateway to the Wakhan. AKDN also supports an ecotourism programme in the Tajik Pamirs, so the intention is to enable adventurous tourists visiting Tajikistan to make a short excursion into Afghan Wakhan. Afghan visas can be easily obtained at the Afghan consulate in Khorog, the capital of Gorno-Badakhshan.

Tourists won't be flocking to Afghanistan in the near future, but as the country seeks to build a more secure and prosperous future, many Afghans are eager to welcome foreign visitors back to their country. Now is the time to begin preparing.

The research on which this paper is based was originally carried out for the purpose of preparing a case study of ecotourism in the Ngorongoro Conservation Area to be used in a course on sustainable tourism offered by the Graduate School of Business at Stanford University. The Business School directed me to base the case study on existing literature and three days of supplemental interviews in the field with key stakeholders. I spent eight days in January 2003 conducting semi-structured interviews in the Ngorongoro Conservation Area and in Arusha with people representing a cross-section of lodges, tourism operators, the NCAA, and NCA Maasai organizations. I interviewed a total of 14 people using both English and Kiswahili. I felt that the effort I invested in synthesizing the literature and thinking about the issue of ecotourism in the NCA; the minimal treatment of this topic in the substantial anthropological literature from the NCA; and the need for a broader critical discussion of the role of ecotourism in conservation and development in the anthropological literature warranted a publication on the topic. However, my methodology was limited by the original scope and purpose of the study. My observations are therefore based largely on a synthesis of the existing literature, supplemented by a rapid rural appraisal conducted in the field. My hope is that this initial summary will stimulate more in depth future research on this topic.

The Ngorongoro Conservation Area covers an area of 8,292 sq. km. in northern Tanzania (Figure 1) (MNRT and NCAA 1996). It forms a part of the greater Serengeti-Mara ecosystem which, as defined by the annual migrations of some 3 million ungulates, spans roughly 25,000 km. sq. in northern Tanzania and southwestern Kenya, and is one of the most important wildlife regions in the world (Homewood and Rodgers 1991:8). Together with the adjacent Serengeti National Park, the NCA has the world's highest density of large mammal species (MNRT and NCAA 1996). The NCA also contains the Ngorongoro Crater, the most famous feature within the Ngorongoro Conservation

Area. Ngorongoro Crater is the largest unbroken caldera in the world, and is one of the best places in Africa to view wildlife (WHSPAPT 2002). In addition, the NCA contains two of the world's richest paleontological and archaeological sites (the Laetoli site and Olduvai Gorge), which span a period of 3.5 million years in human evolution.

Ecotourism is one of the fastest growing segments of the travel industry today. It is potentially an economic alternative or complement to other land-use options, including logging, oil production or cattle ranching. and can represent an important source of foreign exchange.

Many ecotourist destinations in the developing world are located in wilderness areas inhabited by indigenous populations. The rain forests of Brazil, Ecuador and Peru, for example, are home to peoples who depend on the forest for food, building materials and medicine. For years, indigenous people have been competing for resources with large-scale users. The timber and oil industries as well as pharmaceutical companies looking for new drug sources have been encouraged by governments which are struggling to generate foreign exchange. Ecotourism is one of the newest opportunities for income generation from natural resources.

Ecotourism can mean many things to the local people who inhabit these areas -job opportunities, enormous increases in income and a revival of traditional crafts. But it also can have negative social impacts by causing competition for land and resources as well as a disruption of centuries-old values and traditions as wealthy outsiders visit and thereby influence traditional villages and land-use patterns.

Although there are still many unanswered questions about what constitutes proper management, ecotourism does seem to offer a sustainable economic alternative - the possibility of generating income without destroying the environment. However, for ecotourism to work effectively, local people must be partners in the process and derive genuine economic benefit.

Unfortunately, the burgeoning ecotourism industry shows little evidence of local benefit and almost no local control. In the vast majority of cases, ecotourism programmes are run by large national or international companies operating from the capital cities. In many cases, very little of the money generated even enters the country. Local people are often reduced to taking the menial jobs of housekeepers at tourist lodges, cooks and guides. Although some individuals may benefit, the communities as a whole generally do not.

An example of a programme that does not fit this mould is Capirona, an ecotourism effort completely operated by an indigenous community in Ecuador's Amazon basin. Capirona is a community of 24 Quichua Indian families who inhabit the rain forest in Ecuador's Napo Province.

Traditionally, like most indigenous communities in the area, the inhabitants of Capirona have survived by growing subsistence crops and a few hectares of maize and coffee for sale in the market towns up-river.

In the face of steady increases in the price of seeds and transport, several years ago the community was forced to seek other income-producing activities. Unlike recent immigrants into the area, the people of Capirona did not want to turn to logging. They value the forest highly as a source of everything, from food to medicine, and were concerned that logging, although providing short-term gains, might not be managed in a sustainable manner. In an effort to keep this valuable resource intact, in 1991 the community decided collectively to start a small-scale ecotourism programme.

The idea for the project originated with marquises Tapuy, a young man from the village whose elder brother had been the first president of the Confederation of Indigenous Nationalities of Ecuador (CONAIE). The younger Tapuy, concerned that too many young people equated economic success with urban jobs, was committed to starting a successful grassroots development project that would benefit and involve all members of the community. Although, initially, many of the villagers were reluctant to invite outsiders to Capirona, one of the factors that convinced them to change their minds was that travel agents from the town were already bringing tourists into their forest with no direct benefit to the community.

Tapuy, his sister Bertha and Cesar Andy, the former village president, persuaded the community that a small-scale, well-planned project could be minimally intrusive, could generate much-needed income and give them control over who visited their forest. Through a series of community meetings, the villagers worked out the details of the programme and plans for the visitor facilities. With a small loan for the purchase of materials from the indigenous federation of Napo Province, FOIN, and money they had earned from selling maize, they purchased the materials to build a visitors' centre.

Although many families in Capirona aspire to live in tin-roofed, cinder-block structures like their local community centre, they recognized the tourists' desire for "authenticity" and built a small tourist lodge and dining area in the traditional grass and bamboo style with a lovely view of the river. Everyone in the village participated in the construction of the tourist facilities which are a short walk from the main village centre.

From the beginning, it was clear that Capirona would appeal to a special kind of tourist. The community is located on the banks of the River Puni, deep in primary lowland tropical forest in eastern Ecuador. The only access is by foot or dugout canoe when the river is high enough. Visitors are met in the regional capital of Tena and transported to the trail head by truck or bus. From there, they must be able to make the two-hour walk through the forest to the village.

With the help of a German non-governmental organization, Capirona printed flyers about the programme and distributed them in the provincial capital, Tena. The first visitors to Capirona came in groups of two or three -mainly student travellers. In the first year Capirona had fewer than 50 visitors, with a group of four being the largest. Now they are opting for larger groups, arranged in cooperation with study groups from United States universities.

A four- to six-day programme is offered to visitors. Activities include walks in the forest led by guides who recount myths and legends of the forest and explain traditional uses of the vast array of tropical plants and flowers that grow in such profusion; demonstrations of traditional resource use such as basket-making and how to use a blowgun, and participation in the minga, a day when visitors and residents alike share in a communal work project. The minga could be a day clearing the land for planting yucca, constructing a community centre or building a village latrine.

While locally grown maize, yucca and tropical fruits are served to visitors, a large part of the food and supplies must be transported from Tena, several hours up-river by canoe. The community is considering what other food crops could be grown locally to avoid the heavy expense of having to purchase and transport supplies.

The project continues to be a communal effort. Women from different families rotate the responsibility of preparing meals for visitors. Men from the village operate the canoes and act as guides through the forest. Some individuals are responsible for keeping accounts while others monitor supplies. Even the village shaman participates by sharing his special knowledge of the forest, local legends and demonstrating some of the traditional ceremonies. Everyone joins in the farewell party for visitors. Since the programme's emphasis is on cultural exchange, visitors are asked to share something of their culture at the farewell party where traditional Quichua music and dance are offered.

Community members also manage the accounts, determine how much to charge, decide what groups to receive and when and, most important, decide together how to utilize the financial gains. Profits from the project have paid for medical emergencies, provided loans to community members, purchased an outboard motor for the communal canoe and capitalized a small store that sells basic staples to visitors and community members.

A Capirona guide explains the traditional use of plants to a visitor

Code for the Indigenous-sensitive Ecotourist

Ecotourism programmes take place in lands inhabited by indigenous people. An too often, tour groups visit local villages without the permission of, or direct benefit to, the communities involved. Even if a few individuals receive payment for allowing visitors to enter their homes and to take photographs, there is no benefit to the community at large, a situation which may give rise to intracommunity tension.

The following "Code" is based on visitors' guidelines established at Capirona during the 1992 workshop.

Before you visit indigenous areas, whether with a tour or independently, consider the following:

- Who operates the programme? Is it run by local people? If so, is it operated communally or do only a few individuals or families profit?
- If it is not operated by indigenous people, do local communities receive an equitable share of the profits or any other direct benefits, such as training? Or do only a few individuals/families benefit?
- Learn as much as you can about the local culture and customs. Visit local indigenous federation offices for information and materials with an indigenous perspective.
- Do not take photographs without asking permission.
- If you want to give a gift, make it a useful gift to the community rather than to an individual. Most indigenous

communities function communally. Gifts for the local school are much appreciated and shared by all.

- Refrain from tipping individuals. If you are with a group, everyone can contribute to a gift for the community.
- Be aware of the boundaries of individual homes and gardens. Never enter or photograph without permission.
- Bring your own water purification tablets. Do not rely on boiling water exclusively as it depletes scarce fuelwood or contributes to forest destruction.
- Take out what you take in (especially non-biodegradable items such as plastic water bottles). Use biodegradable soaps.
- Be sensitive to those around you. Use headphones with tape/cassette players.
- Do not make promises you cannot or will not keep - for example, sending back photographs to local people.
- Do not collect plants or plant products without permission.
- Wear appropriate and discreet clothing. For example, many cultures are offended by women in shorts even though they may go topless.
- Respect local residents' privacy and customs. Treat people with the same respect you would expect from visitors to your own home.

Refining the Process

In the summer of 1992, the community invited a small team from the University of California Research Expeditions Program (UREP) to organize a workshop that would work with the Capirona community to develop long-term management strategies for the project. The community was particularly concerned about practical issues, so a considerable amount of time was devoted to designing a promotional plan and new brochure; a cost-benefit analysis to determine a pricing structure and the ideal group size; a very basic accounting system; written guidelines for guides and visitors; and suggestions for dealing with emergencies and taking reservations. Workshop members also created a self-guiding trail identifying important local plants, their traditional use and the name in Quichua, Spanish, English and Latin. A second workshop in 1993 initiated a forest and floral survey and also produced trilingual (Quichua, Spanish, English) informational displays for visitors on Quichua history, culture, traditional resource use and the political organization of Ecuador's indigenous groups. Similar displays were created for a regional office in Tena.

Other income-generating activities related to the ecotourism programme were discussed, such as selling locally made crafts, postcards and a biodegradable soap made from a local plant. There was general agreement that the community could not rely on ecotourism alone, but ought to consider other economic alternatives. Some of the possibilities discussed included raising chickens for visitors' meals and selling the surplus in town, establishing Capirona as a guide training centre for the region; and cultivating cacao, natural pesticides or other forest products for sale in Tena.

The workshop in August 1993 further developed some of these ideas, evaluated progress to date, produced a bilingual educational display and began a comprehensive forest survey. The workshop discussions raised many issues about the environmental impact of having visitors. For example, the river is currently used by villagers and visitors both as a water source and for washing and bathing. This situation poses potential problems of river water contamination.

A second challenge was the increasing need to cut wood to sustain the fires that are built several times daily to purify drinking water for visitors. Although the community is now using gas canisters for fuel to boil water, there are questions about the long-term sustainability of this option'. Food was another issue. Locally grown fruits and vegetables comprise the major part of the meals offered to visitors, although supplementary food is purchased and transported from Tena. Given the costs and problems of transport, increasing numbers of visitors may result in clearing more land to produce enough crops to sustain the ecotourism programme. Waste disposal was another consideration in terms of having many visitors over an extended period. The limits needed to safeguard the conservation of the natural resources on which the community depends are still to be determined.

There are also issues of privacy as well as safety. The hard-core ecotourist wants to visit the forest, experience its solitude and wander its paths freely. Yet the forest has many risks for the inexperienced visitor and a guide is necessary for both information and safety. Many ecotourists also want to visit traditional homes and experience a different culture. Yet the Quichua Indians are a private people who are not used to outsiders, much less Westerners. A balance must be established which sets limits on visitors while not making them feel confined or too controlled. The participation of two Native American students (Hopi and Navajo) in the workshops provided an added level of cultural exchange. They shared valuable information on how the Hopi and Navajo have attempted to balance these conflicting interests within their own communities.

Candles for the Tourists, Electricity for the Quichua

The visitors' hut at Capirona has candle lighting, while generators are used for village functions. This dichotomy typifies one of the most serious issues arising from the project: the issue of cultural authenticity. Should the villagers continue to live in traditional huts or wear traditional dress in order to maintain the appearance of "authenticity" to please visitors? Just how far should the community go to accommodate the visitors' desires without compromising their own integrity? Is their traditional culture enhanced by the tourists' interest?

Some claim that tourism revives and maintains traditions that would otherwise be lost, be they traditional dances, ceremonies or crafts. Conversely, maintaining the aura of traditions such as candies for the tourists when the local people want and use lights from generators is unauthentic, because indigenous people are now, and have always been, changing. They do wear Western clothes, many attend school, and all are involved in the struggle to maintain authority over their traditional lands in the face of encroachments ranging from colonists to oil companies. In fact, the future of Capirona's model programme has recently been threatened by the visit of seismic teams from the national oil company exploring for oil in the region. The community adamantly protested this incursion into their lands and, at least for now, the exploratory efforts have ceased.

The enthusiasm of the representatives from nearby villages for starting their own ecotourism projects also made it clear that a regional plan is necessary. For indigenous ecotourist programmes to compete successfully with established four operators, there needs to be a regional plan and policies governing relations with outside travel agents. The market for this specialized segment of the ecotourism industry is limited. So developing programmes with different emphases is crucial to avoid saturating the market. For example, some villages may specialize in taking in bird watchers, others might focus on cultural activities while still others might serve as regional research, education or training centres for local and foreign scientists and students. An indigenous ecotourism network is currently being developed, in conjunction with the regional indigenous federation, to coordinate these activities.

There is growing interest in ecotourism among Ecuador's indigenous peoples. Recently, 23 communities organized a formal ecotourism network under the sponsorship of the provincial indigenous federation, FOIN. So far, only two communities apart from Capirona are accepting visitors, but others are actively preparing to do so. In August 1994, 19 communities of the Shuar ethnic group in Pastaza Province agreed to begin their own ecotourism programmes. The national Amazon Indian federation, CONFENIAE, now has a permanent ecotourism staff position.

Although the country's ecotourism programmes are still predominantly run by large national and international companies without indigenous representation, the situation is beginning to change. The government tourism agency, CETUR, has formed a commission charged with developing tourism in Amazonia in cooperation with indigenous federations.

Much of the current interest in ecotourism among indigenous groups stems from a fear of oil development in the region. Serious contamination of rivers and soils in other parts of Ecuador has galvanized most indigenous federations against oil exploitation. However. the government is still actively exploring for oil in Amazonia. Capirona and many other indigenous communities are located within the prospective sites and have already had conflicts with oil exploration teams.

Ecotourism as a conservation strategy is not a panacea. The travel industry is a fragile business. The place that is "in" this year is out of fashion the next. But, even more important for ecotourist sites, whose very remoteness, pristine nature and wildness make them attractive, is the threat of too much success. Ecotourism will not work for every forest. There must be a diversification of sustainable activities. And where local people are involved they must participate fully and gain equitable benefits.

Bhutanese traditional dress is called the gho (men's robes) and kira (women's dress). The women's dress is a length of woven material (kira) that is draped across the body over a blouse, and held in place over the shoulders with silver clasps. A toego (or jacket) is usually worn over the dress.

The man's gho is a stitched robe, which reaches the ground when first worn. This is then pulled up to knee length and tied in place at the waist with a hand-woven belt. Long socks and shoes, or traditional hand made boots complete the attire.

Traditional dress is worn for all formal occasions including working in the office. The Bhutanese wear their best hand-woven ghos and kiras on formal occasions while machine milled traditional clothing is also popular for daily wear.

There has been a revival in interest in the traditional dress largely inspired by the annual national textile competition and shows organised by the Textile Museum. This annual event encourages weavers to design and produce textiles using the season's colours and has helped to make the gho and kira very fashionable especially among the youth.

With all the hype surrounding Eco-tourism it's refreshing to hear an alternative perspective that questions the validity of claims made on the behalf of ecotourism. The author Anita Pleumarom argues that ecotourism can be just as damaging as other forms of more traditional tourism.

The trend towards eco-tourism holidays, presented as sustainable, nature-based and environmentally friendly, is now subject to considerable controversy. It is the tourism industry's fastest growing subsector, with an estimated world-wide annual growth of 10-15%. Governments as well as the tourism industry promote eco-tourism, with its claims of economic and social sensitivity. But there are well-founded concerns that it lacks adequate scientific foundations, and is not viable as a solution to the world's social and environmental problems.

Eco-tourism is an Eco-facade

Many eco-tourism claims concerning its benefits are exaggerated, or owe more to labelling and marketing than genuine sustainability. Not only are such projects repeatedly planned and carried out without local consent and support, but they often threaten local cultures, economies, and natural resource bases. Critics regard eco-tourism as an `eco-facade': a tactic concealing the mainstream tourism industry's consumptive and exploitative practices by `greening' it. Of particular concern is the side stepping of crucial questions in the promotion of eco-tourism, regarding the global economy and widening gap between North and South, particularly in Third World countries. Significant social and political issues such as the maldistribution of resources, inequalities in political representation and power, and the growth of unsustainable consumption patterns are marginalised or ignored.

Environmentally Risky

Eco-tourism may sound benign, but one of its most serious impacts is the expropriation of`virgin' territories - national parks, wildlife parks and other wilderness areas - which are packaged for eco-tourists as the green option. Eco-tourism is highly consumer-centered, catering mostly to urbanised societies and the new middle-class `alternative lifestyles'. Searching for `untouched' places `off the beaten track' of mass tourism, travellers have already opened up many new destinations.

Mega-resorts, including luxury hotels, condominiums, shopping centres and golf course, are increasingly established in nature reserves in the name of eco-tourism - in many cases protested as `eco-terrorism'. Such projects build completely artificial landscapes, tending to irretrievably wipe out plant and wildlife species - even entire eco-systems.

No Local Benefits

Diverse local social and economic activities are replaced by an eco-tourism monoculture. Contrary to claims, local people do not necessarily benefit from eco-tourism. Tourism-related employment is greatly overrated: locals are usually left with low-paying service jobs such as tour guides, porters, and food and souvenir vendors. In addition, they are not assured of year-round employment: workers may be laid off during the off-season. Most money, as with conventional tourism, is made by foreign airlines, tourism operators, and developers who repatriate profit to their own economically more advanced countries.

Romantic Devastation

Eco-tourism's claim that it preserves and enhances local cultures is highly insincere. Ethnic groups are viewed as a major asset in attracting visitors; an `exotic' backdrop to natural scenery and wildlife. The simultaneous romanticism and devastation of indigenous cultures is one of eco-tourism's ironies. Given a lack of success stories, and sufficient evidence of serious adverse effects, the current huge investments in eco-tourism are misplaced and irresponsible. Research, education, and information for tourists is needed, and the countering of eco-tourism's demeaning of local cultures. - Third World Network Features/African Agenda. The International Ecotourism Society (TIES), founded in 1991, with its headquarters at Burlington, Vermont, U.S., and with global network of about 1,600 members in 110 countries, defines ecotourism as "responsible travel to natural areas that conserve the environment and sustain the well-being of local people". The term "ecotourism" was coined in 1983 by the Mexican architect-environmentalist Hertor Caballos Lascurain, who today is an international consultant on the subject. Ecotourism and its ethics (eco-ethics) are environment and culture-specific.

Traditional or conventional tourism of the past had more of a negative impact, ignoring the sanctity of local environment, biodiversity and indigenous people. For instance, in some Indian wildlife sanctuaries, tourists, often travel in overloaded and rickety vans, that belch thick exhaust while the passengers play loud music. At the sight of wildlife like elephants, they even burst crackers! Film-shooting camps in such sanctuaries are, unfortunately, permitted for days together. Picniking, cooking in the open and disposing of refuse along with polythene bags, and even throwing away unextinguished cigarette butts may kindle forest fires. Some even paint their names on rocks or etch/carve them on tree trunks. Students collect plant or insect specimens for their records. Disorderly and drunken behaviour, nudism and photographing indigenous people without their consent, particularly when they are naked or semi-naked are totally unethical tourist activities that are indulged in.

Responsible tourism observes basic eco-ethical tenets. Fundamental rights like the right to exist or to live in peace, right to pure air and pure water are basic rights even for wildlife, indigenous people as well as for nature as a whole. We must tread on nature softly with reverential silence. Every stone turned over, every log rolled off and leaf-litter swept away, treading on vegetation and trampling in water disturbs habitats and species. Ecotourists should remind themselves of what an American Indian chief wrote in 1854, "We are part of the earth and it is part of us,... . This shining water that moves in the streams and rivers is not just water, but the blood of our ancestors,... The water's murmur is the voice of my father's father. Nature tourism and wildlife tourism are top priority for most tourists, but in the Indian context, all picnics, nature walks, nature camps, trekking, hiking, safaris, jungle trails, mountaineering, cultural tours, pilgrimages (yatras), beaching, water sports, canoeing, boating and game-fishing should all observe eco-ethics. One step forward in ecotourism is to get involved in eco-restoration, biodiversity restoration and eco-development of local people in any degraded tourist ecosystem.

India, with her kaleidoscopic ecosystems and a wealth of cultural heritages of great antiquity, has immense scope for ecotourism. Constant research to identify newer areas and spots for ecotourism, preparing brochures on them and on the eco-ethics relevant to each, organising environmental trails and training knowledgeable guides, preferably using the services of local people, are the obligations of the tourism department.

The Government should liberalise several infrastructural constraints facing foreign ecotourists to India. Managers of tourist areas and spots should provide basic services to ecotourists through educational centres on the spot, supplying information brochures and selling eco-friendly souvenirs. The sale of local plant and animal products should be strictly banned and conscientious ecotourists will not buy them. Eco-friendly handicraft items made by indigenous people could be purchased as gestures to encourage their welfare. The lack of even adequate rest areas with clean rest rooms (toilet facilities) is a serious lacuna in Indian tourism. "Ecolodges", with food, drinking water, telephone and e-mail facilities and shopping centres for essentials would be added tourist amenities. Admitting ecotourists upto the "carrying capacity" of the area and maintaining security to check on violations are advisable. Collection of much needed data in India from ecotourists will help to improve the management a lot. Charging a suitable entrance fee to all ecotourist areas and spots to meet the costs of services and conservation is not out of the way. This novel concept of ecotourism is so visionary that in the long run, it would be much more viable economically, sustainable ecologically, acceptable socially and ideal philosophically than traditional tourism.

Ecotourism (also known as ecological tourism) is travel to fragile, pristine, and usually protected areas that strives to be low impact and (often) small scale. It helps educate the traveler; provides funds for conservation; directly benefits the economic development and political empowerment of local communities; and fosters respect for different cultures and for human rights.

Ecotourism appeals to ecologically and socially conscious individuals. Generally speaking, it focuses on volunteering, personal growth and learning new ways to live on the planet. It typically involves travel to destinations where flora, fauna, and cultural heritage are the primary attractions. Ecotourism is a conceptual experience, enriching those who delve into researching and understanding the environment around them. It gives us insight into our impacts as human beings and also a greater appreciation of our own natural habitats. Responsible Ecotourism includes programs that minimize the negative aspects of conventional tourism on the environment and enhance the cultural integrity of local people. Therefore, in addition to evaluating environmental and cultural factors, an integral part of ecotourism is the promotion of recycling, energy efficiency, water conservation and creation of economic opportunities for the local communities.

Understanding Sustainable Tourism: Sustainable tourism is a kind of approach to tourism meant to make the development of tourism ecologically supportable in the long term. The very importance of sustainable tourism lies in its motives to conserve the resources and increase the value of local culture and tradition. Sustainable tourism is a responsible tourism intending to generate employment and income along with alleviating any deeper impact on environment and local culture.

Relationship Between Ecotourism and Sustainable Tourism

Ecotourism basically deals with nature based tourism, and is aimed "to conserve the environment and improves the well-being of local people". On the other hand, sustainable tourism includes all segments of tourism, and has same function to perform as of ecotourism - to conserve the resources and increase the local cultural and traditional value. Though the goals of ecotourism and sustainable tourism is much similar, but the latter is broader and conceals within itself very many aspects and categories of tourism.

So, Step out of your SUVs and get a glimpse of the scenic surrounding on a traditional bullock cart. And, you are even entitled to a bullock cart driving licence after a few basic lessons.

You could even try your hand at ploughing a field with the help of a trained instructor. And that's not all! At Our Native Village you get the opportunity to milk a cow or work on an organic farm other than bicycle rides, nature treks, heritage tours.

Chapter-3

Animal Watching in Their Natural Habitat

India has some of the world's most biodiverse regions. The political boundaries of India encompass a wide range of ecozones-desert, high mountains, highlands, tropical and temperate forests, swamplands, plains, grasslands, areas surrounding rivers, as well as island archipelago. It hosts three biodiversity hotspots: the Western Ghats, the Eastern Himalayas, and the hilly ranges that straddle the India-Myanmar border. These hotspots have numerous endemic species.

India, for the most part, lies within the Indomalaya ecozone, with the upper reaches of the Himalayas forming part of the Palearctic ecozone; the contours of 2000 to 2500m are considered to be the altitudinal boundary between the Indo-Malayan and Palearctic zones. India displays significant biodiversity. One of eighteen megadiverse countries, it is home to 7.6% of all mammalian, 12.6% of all avian, 6.2% of all reptilian, 4.4% of all amphibian, 11.7% of all fish, and 6.0% of all flowering plant species. The region is also heavily influenced by summer monsoons that cause major seasonal changes in vegetation and habitat. India forms a large part of the Indomalayan biogeographical zone and many of the floral and faunal forms show Malayan affinities with only a few taxa being unique to the Indian region. The unique forms includes the snake family Uropeltidae found only in the Western Ghats and

Sri Lanka. Fossil taxa from the Cretaceous show links to the Seychelles and Madagascar chain of islands. The Cretaceous fauna include reptiles, amphibians and fishes and an extant species demonstrating this phylogeographical link is the Purple Frog. The separation of India and Madagascar is traditionally estimated to have taken place about 88 million years ago. However there are suggestions that the links to Madagascar and Africa were present even at the time when the Indian subcontinent met Eurasia. India has been suggested as a ship for the movement of several African taxa into Asia. These taxa include five frog families (including the Myobatrachidae), three caecilian families, a lacertid lizard and freshwater snails of the family Potamiopsidae. A fossil tooth of what is believed to be of from a lemur-like primate from the Bugti Hills of central Pakistan however has led to suggestions that the lemurs may have originated in Asia. These fossils are however from the Oligocene (30 million years ago) and have led to controversy. Lemur fossils from India in the past led to theories of a lost continent called Lemuria. This theory however was dismissed when continental drift and plate tectonics became well established.

The flora and fauna of India have been studied and recorded from early times in folk traditions and later by researchers following more formal scientific approaches (See Natural history in India). Game laws are reported from the third century BC.

A little under 5% of this total area is formally classified under protected areas.

India is home to several well known large mammals including the Asian Elephant, Bengal Tiger, Asiatic Lion, Leopard and Indian Rhinoceros. Some of these animals are engrained in culture, often being associated with deities. These large mammals are important for wildlife tourism in India and several national parks and wildlife sanctuaries cater to these needs. The popularity of these charismatic animals have helped greatly in conservation efforts in India. The tiger has been particularly important and Project Tiger started in 1972 was a major effort to conserve the tiger and its habitats. Project Elephant, though less known, started in 1992 and works for elephant protection. Most of India's rhinos today survive in the Kaziranga National Park. Other well known large Indian mammals include ungulates such as the Water Buffalo, Nilgai, Gaur and several species of deer and antelope. Some members of the dog family such as the Indian Wolf, Bengal Fox, Golden Jackal and the Dhole or Wild Dogs are also widely distributed. It is also home to the Striped Hyaena. Many smaller animals such as the Macaques, Langurs and Mongoose species are especially well known due to their ability to live close to or inside urban areas.

The Western Ghats

The Western Ghats are a chain of hills that run along the western edge of peninsular India. Their proximity to the ocean and through orographic effect, they receive high rainfall. These regions have moist deciduous forest and rain forest. The region shows high species diversity as well as high levels of endemism. Nearly 77% of the amphibians and 62% of the reptile species found here are found nowhere else. The region shows biogeographical affinities to the Malayan region, and the Satpura hypothesis proposed by Sunder Lal Hora suggests that the hill chains of Central India may have once formed a connection with the forests of northeastern India and into the Indo-Malayan region. Hora used torrent stream fishes to support the theory, but it was also suggested to hold for birds. Later studies have suggested that Hora's original model species were a demonstration of convergent evolution rather than speciation by isolation.

More recent phylogeographic studies have attempted to study the problem using molecular approaches. There are also differences in taxa which are dependent on time of divergence and geological history. Along with Sri Lanka this region also shows some faunal similarities with the Madagascan region especially in the reptiles and amphibians. Examples include the Sibynophis snakes, the Purple frog and Sri Lankan lizard genus Nessia which appears similar to the Madagascan genus Acontias. Numerous floral links to the Madagascan region also exist. An alternate hypothesis that these taxa may have originally evolved out-of-India has also been suggested.

Biogeographical quirks exist with some taxa of Malayan origin occurring in Sri Lanka but absent in the Western Ghats. These include insects groups such as the zoraptera and plants such as those of the genus Nepenthes.

The Eastern Himalayas

The Eastern Himalayas is the region encompassing Bhutan, northeastern India, and southern, central, and eastern Nepal. The region is geologically young and shows high altitudinal variation. It has nearly 163 globally threatened species including the One-horned Rhinoceros (Rhinoceros unicornis), the Wild Asian Water buffalo (Bubalus bubalis (Arnee)) and in all 45 mammals, 50 birds, 17 reptiles, 12 amphibians, 3 invertebrate and 36 plant species. The Relict Dragonfly (Epiophlebia laidlawi) is an endangered species found here with the only other species in the genus being found in Japan. The region is also home to the Himalayan Newt (Tylototriton verrucosus), the only salamander species found within Indian limits.

Extinct and Fossil Forms

During the early Tertiary period, the Indian tableland, what is today peninsular India, was a large island. Prior to becoming an island it was connected to the African region. During the tertiary period this island was separated from the Asian mainland by a shallow sea. The Himalayan region and the greater part of Tibet lay under this sea. The movement of the Indian subcontinent into the Asian landmass created the great Himalayan ranges and raised the sea bed into what is today the plains of northern India.

Once connected to the Asian mainland, many species moved into India. The Himalayas were created in several upheavals. The Siwaliks were formed in the last and the largest number of fossils of the Tertiary period are found in these ranges.

The Siwalik fossils include Mastodons, hippopotamus, rhinoceros, Sivatherium, a large four-horned ruminant, giraffe, horses, camels, bison, deer, antelope, pigs, chimpanzees, orangutans, baboons, langurs, macaques, cheetahs, sabre-toothed cats, lions, tigers, sloth bear, Aurochs, leopards, wolves, dholes, porcupines, rabbits and a host of other mammals.

Many fossil tree species have been found in the intertrappean beds including Grewioxylon from the Eocene and Heritieroxylon keralensis from the middle Miocene in Kerala and Heritieroxylon arunachalensis from the Mio-Pliocene of Arunachal Pradesh and at many other places. The discovery of Glossopteris fern fossils from India and Antarctica led to the discovery of Gondwanaland and led to the greater understanding of continental drift. Fossil Cycads are known from India while seven Cycad species continue to survive in India.

Titanosaurus indicus was perhaps the first dinosaur discovered in India by Richard Lydekker in 1877 in the Narmada valley. This area has been one of the most important areas for paleontology in India. Another dinosaur known from India is Rajasaurus narmadensis , a heavy-bodied and stout carnivorous abelisaurid (theropod) dinosaur that inhabited the area near present-day Narmada river. It was 9 m in length and 3 m in height and somewhat horizontal in posture with a double-crested crown on the skull.

Some fossil snakes from the Cenozoic era are also known. Some scientists have suggested that the Deccan lava flows and the gases produced were responsible for the global extinction of dinosaurs however these have been disputed. Himalayacetus subathuensis the oldest-known whale fossil of the family

Protocetidae (Eocene), about 53.5 million years old was found in the Simla hills in the foothills of the Himalayas. This area was underwater (in the Tethys sea) during the Tertiary period (when India was an island off Asia). This whale may have been capable of living partly on land. Other fossil whales from India include Remingtonocetus approximately 43-46 million years old.

Several small mammal fossils have been recorded in the intertrappean beds, however larger mammals are mostly unknown. The only major primate fossils have been from the nearby region of Myanmar.

Recent Extinctions

The exploitation of land and forest resources by humans along with hunting and trapping for food and sport has led to the extinction of many species in India in recent times.

Probably the first species to vanish during the time of the Indus Vally civilisation was the species of wild cattle, Bos primegenius nomadicus or the wild zebu, which vanished from its range in the Indus valley and western India, possibly due to inter-breeding with domestic cattle and resultant fragmentation of wild populations due to loss of habitat.

Notable mammals which became or are presumed extinct within the country itself include the Indian / Asiatic Cheetah, Javan Rhinoceros and Sumatran Rhinoceros. While some of these large mammal species are confirmed extinct, there have been many smaller animal and plant species whose status is harder to determine. Many species have not been seen since their description. Hubbardia heptaneuron, a species of grass that grew in the spray zone of the Jog Falls prior to the construction of the Linganamakki reservoir, was thought to be extinct but a few were rediscovered near Kolhapur.

Some species of birds have gone extinct in recent times, includinq the Pink-Headed Duck (Rhodonessa caryophyllacea) and the Himalayan Quail (Ophrysia superciliosa). A species of warbler, Acrocephalus orinus, known earlier from a single specimen collected by Allan Octavian Hume from near Rampur in Himachal Pradesh was rediscovered after 139 years in Thailand. Similarly, the Jerdon's Courser (Rhinoptilus bitorquatus), named after the zoologist Thomas C. Jerdon who discovered it in 1848, was rediscovered in 1986 by Bharat Bhushan, an ornithologist at the Bombay Natural History Society after being thought to be extinct.

Species Estimates

An estimate of the numbers of species by group in India is given below. This is based on Alfred, 1998.

Taxonomic Group	World species	Indian species	% in India
PROTISTA			
Protozoa	31250	2577	8.24
Total (Protista)	31250	2577	8.24
ANIMALIA			
Mesozoa	71	10	14.08
Porifera	4562	486	10.65
Cnidaria	9916	842	8.49
Ctenophora	100	12	12
Platyhelminthes	17500	1622	9.27
Nemertinea	600		
Rotifera	2500	330	13.2
Gastrotricha	3000	100	3.33
Kinorhyncha	100	10	10
Nematoda	30000	2850	9.5
Nematomorpha	250		
Acanthocephala	800	229	28.62

Sipuncula	145	35	24.14
Mollusca	66535	5070	7.62
Echiura	127	43	33.86
Annelida	12700	840	6.61
Onychophora	100	1	1
Arthropoda	987949	68389	6.9
Crustacea	35534	2934	8.26
Insecta			6.83
Arachnida	73440		7.9
Pycnogonida	600		2.67
Pauropoda	360		
Chilopoda	3000	100	3.33
Diplopoda	7500	162	2.16
Symphyla	120	4	3.33
Merostomata	4	2	50
Phoronida	11	3	27.27
Bryozoa (Ectoprocta)	4000	200	5
Endoprocta	60	10	16.66
Brachiopoda	300	3	1
Pogonophora	80		
Praipulida	8		
Pentastomida	70		
Chaetognatha	111	30	27.02
Tardigrada	514	30	5.83
Echinodermata	6223	765	12.29
Hemichordata	120	12	10
Chordata	48451	4952	10.22
Protochordata			
(Cephalochordata+			

Urochordata)	2106	119	5.65
Pisces	21723	2546	11.72
Amphibia	5150	209	4.06
Reptilia	5817	456	7.84
Aves	9026	1232	13.66
Mammalia	4629	390	8.42
Total (Animalia)	1196903	868741	7.25
Grand Total (Protosticta+ Animalia)	1228153	871318	7.09

This section provides links to lists of species of various taxa found in India.

Animals

Invertebrates

- Molluscs

  List of non-marine molluscs of India
- Arachnids

  Spiders of India
- Insects

  Coccinellidae
- Ladybird beetles of India

  Odonata
- Dragonflies and damselflies of India

  Lepidoptera
- Butterflies of India
- Papilionid butterflies of India
- Pierid butterflies of India

- Nymphalid butterflies of India
- Lycaenid butterflies of India
- Hesperid butterflies of India
- Riodinid butterflies of India
- Moths of India

Hymenoptera

- Ants of India

Vertebrates

- Fishes of India
- Amphibians of India
- Reptiles of India

Snakes of India

- Birds of South Asia
- Mammals of India

Plants

See Flora of India

Threatened species

Many plants and animals are threatened or endangered due largely to habitat loss and population pressure apart from hunting and extraction. India stands out as one of the few countries with high human populations as well as a high number of threatened species.

Threatened plant species

Threat Category (IUCN)	Number of species
Extinct	19
Extinct/Endangered	43
Endangered	149

Endangered/Vulnerable	2
Vulnerable	108
Rare	256
Indeterminate	719
Insufficiently Known	9
No information	1441
Not threatened	374
TOTAL	**3120**

Karnala bird sanctuary is located on NH 7, Mumbai-Goa Highway about 50 km from Mumbai and 17 km from Panvel.The Karnala bird sanctuary and fort is a perfect day trip from fast paced Mumbai. You can go in the morning and back home by evening. Karnala is a popular destination for birdwatchers as well as favourite rock climbing spot. This is a small sanctuary with just 4.27 sqkm of land. But it is home to 147 species of resident and 37 species of migratory birds that come during winter. Two rare birds ashy minivet and the Malabar trogon have been spotted here.

The monsoons transform this place with green dominating the landscape. There is freshness in the air with trees blooming with new leaves. The sanctuary is also favourite of the trekkers. There is fortress within the sanctuary. Its construction is believed to date the 12th century and over the sanctuaries changed many rulers and dynasties. In 1818 the fort was captured by Colonel Prother who established the East India Company rule. The fort has a series of ornate steps leading to higher section of the fort. The 45 m basalt pillar was once used as a watchtower now it serves as a challenge to rock climbers. The best time to visit it is in monsoon or around November.

Parambikulam Wildlife Sanctuary is tucked away in the valley between the Anamala ranges of Tamil Nadu and the Nelliampathy ranges of Kerala on the majestic Western Ghats. It is home to varied wildlife such as bonnet macque,lion tailed macaque,Nilgiri langur,leopard,civit Nilgiri Tahr,spotted deer,sambar.Different species of snakes are also located here with king cobra, spectacled cobra,krait,viper,python,rat snake, vine snake etc. There are wide varieties of birds such as aral, bral, thilopia, taral etc with black eagle, black capped kingfisher, great Indian hornbill, broad billed roller, black woodpecker etc.The location of the sanctuary offers the unique advantage of watching the fascinating wildlife from close quarters.The lush green flora is breath-taking with fresh air .

Bheemeshwari Wildlife Sanctuary is a perfect picnic spot where nature has created a natural habitat for the Mahseer fish and variety of other animals. The lush green forest sheltered by steep valley and scattered by little streams invite large group of animals and birds which includes elephants, deer, wild boars, monkeys, jackals, crocodiles and leopards. There are wide varieties of birds like heron, ibis, cormorant, kingfishers which have made their home here. Angling is an exciting option here as there is a fishing camp nearby. The river Cauvery abounds with Mahseer -the finest game fish. The best time to visit is from December to March.

The Similipal National Park is one of the earliest parks to come under Project Tiger. It is located in the forest belt of north Orissa. It was the erstwhile hunting preserve of the Maharajas of Mayurbanj.Similipal covering an area of 2750 sq kms was declared in 1973 as one of the nine Project Tiger reserves in the country. It is a vast tract of stately sal forests with beautiful waterfalls, grassy valley and twelve rivers run across its expanse.Similipal tiger reserve is home to panthers, tigers, gaur, bisons, antelopes, sambar, mouse deer the tiniest of the deer family. There are more than 223 species of birds. Permits are needed to obtain prior to the visit to the tiger reserve. The best time to visit is from October to early June.

Chilika Lake spreading over an area of 1100 sq km is the largest brackish water lake in the country. It attracts a large number of migratory birds besides resident ones.Barkul and Rambha are two places on the lake which serve as the base. The Dolphins have been reported mostly near Satapada-Magarmukha area and occasionally between Kalijai and Balugaon.Other animals reported from small pockets in the surrounding hills and islands and amidst the vegetation of sandy ridge facing Chilika are black bucks, spotted deer, jungle cat, otter, and monkeys etc. The best time to visit is from October to early June.

The Neora national park is located in Darjeeling district at the trijunction of Bhutan,West Bengal and Sikkim.The Neora national park is named after the river that flows within the park. The park has a number of torrents and hill streams spread like a net sustaining the river and green vegetation within the protected area. The park has amazing variety of flora like tiny wild strawberries, wild white orchids, primulas to the Himalayan yews and hemlocks. It supports an impressive population of birds and mammals. The park is home to more than 200 species of birds.

The most visible are male satyr trgopan, kalij pheasant, golden eagle, jerdon's baza, nutcracker, magpies and flinches. Animals in the park include the tiger and the leopard among the big cats. While pugmarks of Asiatic bear are common, sightings are rare. The goral and barking deer are easily spotted in the park. Around 10 species of rhododendrons have been recorded here from the scarlet gurans to the milk white chimawl.Visible from the top of the pass is the magnificent Kangchendzonga range. The best time to visit is from March to June and Oct to December. To enter the park one must have permission from the wildlife authorities in Jalpaiguri.

Visit Bharatpur in winter when the Keoladeo Ghana Bird Sanctuary is full of exotic, foreign winged visitors who migrate here from across the globe. Spring is the time for courtship and nesting. The rains are for breeding and rearing young with nests across the parklands brimminq with mottled and speckled eggs of many colours. Once the hunting ground of the Maharaja of Bharatpur the swamps and marshes of the 29 sq km Keoladeo Ghana was later turned into a bird sanctuary and now ranks among the most visited in India.

To get the real joy of the park divide the trips over the different times of the day. Experience the early morning birdlife and exquisite birdsong, see spectacular sightings of large flocks of water birds like ducks,geese,pelicans,flamingos,painted storks and catch the elusive birds at dusk like night herons, bitterns and owls.

The Mansarovar and Hansarovar marshes and the swamps and lakes of Bharatpur constitute one of the most important heronries in the world. For this Keoladeo is a World Heritage Site. The park give good sightings of the slender necked purple heron, the petite brown pond heron, the common pond heron, the common grey heron and several other species. You can also see long toed jacanas walking magically across the water and large flocks of pelicans and flamingos fishing in the deeper waters. In addition to birds there are also sambhar, chital, nilgai and mongoose in the park. If there is enough water tourists can also enjoy boating and admire the birds from a close range.

Periyar is a protected area, and a nature reserve in the South Indian State of Kerala, set high in the mountains of the Western Ghats at the border to Tamil Nadu. It lies in the districts of Idukki and Pathanamthitta. The protected area covers an area of 925 km^2, out of which a 350 km^2 part of the core zone was made into the Periyar National Park and Tiger Reserve, sometimes dubbed the Periyar Wildlife Sanctuary. The park is often called by the name thekkady also. Thekkady is located four km from Kumily, approximately 100 km east of Alappuzha, 110 km west of Madurai and 120 km southeast from Kochi.

The Periyar protected area lies in the middle of a mountainous area of the Cardamom Hills. In the north and the east it is bounded by mountain ridges of over 1700 metres altitude and toward the west it expands into a 1200 meter high plateau. From this level the altitude drops steeply to the deepest point of the reserve, the 100 meter valley of the Pamba River. The highest peak is the 2019 meter high Kottamalai.

The sanctuary surrounds picturesque 26 km² Periyar lake, formed by the building of Mullaperiyar Dam in 1895. This reservoir and the Periyar River meander around the contours of the wooded hills, providing a permanent source of water for the local wildlife.

Climate and Temperature

The temperatures vary depending upon the altitude and it ranges between 15° Celsius in December and January and 31° Celsius in April and May. The annual amount of precipitation lies between 2000 and 3000 mm. About two thirds of the precipitation occurs during the southwest monsoon between June to September. A smaller amount of precipitation occurs during the northeast monsoon between October and December.

Vegetation

Approximately 75% of the entire protected area are covered of unaffected evergreen or semi-evergreen rain forest. There typically tall tropical tree species such as Vateria indica, Cullenia exarillata, Hopea parviflora, Canarium strictum, Artocarpus hirsutus and Bischofia javanica are seen. They reach heights of 40 to 50 Metres.

Scarcely 13% consists of damp leaves forest, 7% of Eucalyptus plantation and 1.5% of grassland. The remainder (around 3.5%) of the protected area is covered by the Periyar artificial lake as well as the Periyar River and Pamba rivers.

Altogether the reservation counts nearly 2000 kinds of flowering plants (Angiosperms), three kinds of seed plants (gymnosperms) and 170 different species of ferns. Among the Angiosperms, there are 169 families of sweet grasses and 155 kinds of Fabaceae. Orchids, with 145 representative types, are the most frequent flower.

About 350 of the occurring plant types can be used for medical purposes.

Fauna

Altogether 62 different kinds of mammal have been recorded in Periyar, including many threatened ones. There are an estimated 53 tigers(2010) in the reserve. Tourists also come here to view the Indian elephants in the act of ablution and playfulness by the Periyar lake. The elephant number around 900 to 1000 individuals. Other mammals found here include gaur, sambar (horse deer), barking deer, mouse deer, Dholes (Indian wild dogs), mongoose, foxes and leopards. Also inhabiting the park, though rarely seen, are the elusive Nilgiri tahr.

Four species of primates are found at Periyar - the rare lion-tailed macaque, the Nilgiri Langur, the common langur, and the Bonnet Macaque.

Birds

So far 320 different kinds have been counted in Periyar. The bird life includes darters, cormorants, kingfishers, the great Malabar hornbill and racket-tailed Drongos.

Reptiles

There are 45 different kinds of reptile in the protected area out of which there are 30 snake, two turtle, and 13 lizard species. Among those are Monitor lizards that can be spotted basking in the sun on the rocks along the lake shore. Visitors who trek into the Periyar national park often see a Python and sometimes even a King Cobra.

Amphibians

Twenty seven different kinds have been recorded, of which ten are endemic to the Western Ghats, such as some species of frogs and cecilians.

Fish

In the waters of the protected area 38 different fish types live, of which four are endemic to the Western Ghats. Salmon,trout is also here.

Insects

There is a remarkable variety of butterflies and there are about 160 different kinds in total. Some are dangerous enough to make a human seriously ill

PERIYAR TIGER RESERVE

Periyar Tiger Reserve is one of the 27 tiger reserves in India. Periyar Tiger Reserve is located in the Western Ghats in Idukki District of the Kerala state in India. The terrain of the Reserve is undulating and the drainage is dendrite. North-eastern boundary of the Reserve is a ridge, which also forms boundary between Kerala and Tamil Nadu states for 90 km.

Its a must to go for Jungle Trek during your visit to the Periyar National Park. There are different kind of options available for the Jungle Trek. There are options available for the short trek of 4 hours starting in morning and afternoon. One can also trek with the night patrol with the forest guard through the jungle, when there are better chances of spotting wildlife from up close.

During the trek the flora and fauna can be experienced at close quarters and if one is lucky enough there are chances to sight the bigger animals of the cat family.

History

The man-made dam which formed Periyar Lake

1895 - Construction of the Mullaperiyar Dam

1899 - Formation of the Periyar Lake Reserve

1933 - S.C.H. Robinson made the first game warden

1934 - Formation of Nellikkampatty Game Sanctuary

1950 - Consolidation of Periyar as a Wildlife sanctuary

1978 - Declaration of Periyar as a Tiger Reserve

1982 - Preliminary notification of the core area as a National Park

1991 - Brought under Project Elephant

1996 - India Ecodevelopment Project launched

2001 - Reorganised as two Divisions: Periyar East and Periyar West

Tourists and Pilgrims

There are allegations that The Periyar tiger reserve is a poorly monitored National park and the welfare of the wildlife has been compromised for the Ecotourism project which is undoubtedly considered to be a commercial success in India. The core zone of the park is not accessible to the tourists. Within the buffer zone of 430 km², a zone of 55 km² is kept apart for tourism. Game wardens and staff have been recently spotted illegally fishing and gathering specimens within the sanctuary area. The facilities within the sanctuary are in need of much maintenance and are presently in very poor standards. This has also contributed a steady decline in returning tourists to the sanctuary.

In the buffer zone there is also the temple of Sabarimala, which is visited by about 4 million pilgrims annually. Its important to recognize, however, that for the very purpose of protecting its wildlife and shielding them from human interference, Periyar National Park allows extremely limited access to the territory under its jurisdiction, restricting tourist entry only to the northern corner adjacent to man-made lake Periyar. Despite this, Park authorities are engaged in a constant struggle against tiger and elephant poachers and other illegal intruders, many of whom destroy the forest to cultivate cannabis in its most inaccessible reaches.

Kanha National park is located in Banjar and Halon valleys in the Mandla / Balaghat districts of the state of Madhya Pradesh. Kanha National Park is one of the India's finest tiger reserves. It is spread more than 940 sq km in a horse shoe shaped valley bound by the spurs of the Mekal range the park presents a varies topography.

Kanha national park is more famous for its wildlife, the natural beauty of its landscape is just as fascinating. One of the best locations to enjoy that bounty is Bammi Dadar, also known as the sunset point..

Kanha also shelters one of the largest populations of the tigers in the country. Some of the other larger animal species found in the park are sloth bear, leopard, striped hyena, spotted dear, wild boar, jungle cat, jackal and a variety of monkeys. Over 200 spices of birds have been spotted in the park. There are many folklore about how it got kanha name. Some say it came from kanha, the clay like soil of the river bottoms, Other say the area is named for kanha a holy forest sage, who once lived here and was the father of shakuntala, whose son was Bharat and whose story was told in our legends.

Jim Corbett National Park-named after the hunter turned conservationist Jim Corbett who played a key role in its establishment-is the oldest national park in India. The park was established in 1936 as Hailey National Park. Situated in Nainital district of Uttarakhand the park acts as a protected area for the critically endangered Bengal tiger of India, the secure survival of which is the main objective of Project Tiger, an Indian wildlife protection initiative.

The park has sub-Himalayan belt geographical and ecological characteristics. An ecotourism destination, it contains 488 different species of plants and a diverse variety of fauna. The increase in tourist activities, among other problems, continues to present a serious challenge to the park's ecological balance.

Corbett has been a haunt for tourists and wildlife lovers for a long time. Tourism activity is only allowed in selected areas of Corbett Tiger Reserve so that people get an opportunity to see its splendid landscape and the diverse wildlife. In recent years the number of people coming here has increased dramatically. Presently, every season more than 70,000 visitors come to the park from India and other countries.

The Jim Corbett National Park is a heaven for the adventure seeker and wildlife adventure lovers. Corbett National Park is India's first national park which comprises 520.8 km2. area of hills, riverine belts, marshy depressions, grass lands and large lake. The elevation ranges from 1,300 feet to 4,000 feet. Winter nights in Corbett national park are cold but the days are bright and sunny. It rains from July to September.

Dense moist deciduous forest mainly consists of sal, haldu, pipal, rohini and mango trees, and these trees cover almost 73 per cent of the park. The 10 per cent of the area consists of grasslands.It houses around 110 tree species, 50 species of mammals, 580 bird species and 25 reptile species. The endangered Bengal tiger of India resides here. The sanctuary was the first to come under Project Tiger initiative.

Some areas of the park were formerly part of the princely state of Tehri Garhwal. The forests were cleared to make the area less vulnerable to Rohilla invaders. The Raja of Tehri formally ceded a part of his princely state to the East India Company in return for their assistance in ousting the Gurkhas from his domain. The Boksas-a tribe from the Terai-settled on the land and began growing crops, but in the early 1860s they were evicted with the advent of British rule. The British forest department established control over the land and prohibited cultivation and the operation of cattle stations. The British administration considered the possibility of creating a game reserve there in 1907 and established a reserve area known as Hailey National Park covering 323.75 km2 (125.00 sq mi) in 1936. The preserve was renamed in 1954-55 as Ramganga National Park and was again renamed in 1955-56 as Corbett National Park. The new name honours the well-known author and wildlife conservationist Jim Corbett, who played a key role in creating the reserve by using his influence to persuade the provincial government to establish it

The reserve does not allow hunting, but does permit timber cutting for domestic purposes. Soon after the establishment of the reserve, rules prohibiting killing and capturing of mammals, reptiles and birds within its boundaries were passed. The park fared well during the 1930s under an elected administration. But during the Second World War, it suffered from excessive poaching and timber cutting. Over time the area in the reserve was increased-797.72 km2 (308.00 sq mi) were added in 1991 as a buffer for the Corbett Tiger Reserve. The 1991 additions included the entire Kalagarh forest division, assimilating the 301.18 km2 (116.29 sq mi) area of Sonanadi Wildlife Sanctuary as a part of the Kalagarh division. It was chosen in 1974 as the location for launching Project Tiger, an ambitious and well known wildlife conservation project. The reserve is administered from its headquarters in the district of Nainital.

Corbett National Park is one of the thirteen protected areas covered by World Wildlife Fund under their Terai Arc Landscape Programme. The programme aims to protect three of the five terrestrial flagship species, the tiger, the Asian elephant and the Great One-horned Rhinoceros, by restoring corridors of forest to link 13 protected areas of Nepal and India to enable wildlife migration.

Geography

The park is located between 29°25' to 29°39'N latitude and 78°44' to 79°07'E longitude. The average altitude of the region ranges between 360 m (1,181 ft) and 1,040 m (3,412 ft). It has numerous ravines, ridges, minor streams and small plateaus with varying aspects and degrees of slopes. The park encompasses the Patli Dun valley formed by the Ramganga river. It protects parts of the Upper Gangetic Plains moist deciduous forests and Himalayan subtropical pine forests ecoregions. It has a humid subtropical and highland climate.

The present area of the Reserve is 1,318.54 square kilometres (509.09 sq mi) including 520 square kilometres (200 sq mi) of core area and 797.72 square kilometres (308.00 sq mi) of buffer area. The core area forms the Jim Corbett National Park while the buffer contains reserve forests (496.54 square kilometres (191.72 sq mi)) as well as the Sonanadi Wildlife Sanctuary 301.18 square kilometres (116.29 sq mi)).

The reserve, located partly along a valley between the Lesser Himalaya in the north and the Siwaliks in the south, has a sub-Himalayan belt structure. The upper tertiary rocks are exposed towards the base of the Siwalik range and hard sandstone units form broad ridges. Characteristic longitudinal valleys, geographically termed Doons, or Duns can be seen formed along the narrow tectonic zones between lineaments. link title

Climate

The weather in the park is temperate compared to most other protected areas of India. The temperature may vary from 5 °C (41 °F) to 30 °C (86 °F) during the winter and some mornings are foggy. Summer temperatures normally do not rise above 40 °C (104 °F). Rainfall ranges from light during the dry season to heavy during the monsoons.

Flora

A total of 488 different species of plants have been recorded in the park. Tree density inside the reserve is higher in the areas of Sal forests and lowest in the Anogeissus-Acacia catechu forests. Total tree basal cover is greater in Sal dominated areas of woody vegetation. Healthy regeneration in sapling and seedling layers is occurring in the Mallotus philippensis, Jamun and Diospyros tomentosa communities, but in the Sal forests the regeneration of sapling and seedling is poor.

Fauna

Little green bee-eaters at Jim Corbett National Park

A bull elephant in Corbett National Park

Over 585 species of resident and migratory birds have been categorized, including the crested serpent eagle, blossom-headed parakeet and the red junglefowl - ancestor of all domestic fowl. 33 species of reptiles, seven species of amphibians, seven species of fish and 37 species of dragonflies have also been recorded.

Bengal tigers, although plentiful, are not easily spotted due to the abundance of camouflage in the reserve. Thick jungle, the Ramganga river, and plentiful prey make this reserve an ideal habitat for tigers who are opportunistic feeders and prey upon a range of animals. The tigers in the park have been known to kill much larger animals such as buffalo and even elephant for food. The tigers prey upon the larger animals in rare cases of food shortage. There have been incidents of tigers attacking domestic animals in times when there is a shortage of prey.

Spotted Deer at Jim Corbett

Leopards are found in hilly areas but may also venture into the low land jungles. Smaller felines in the park include the jungle cat, fishing cat and leopard cat. Other mammals include four kinds of deer (barking, sambar, hog, Black buck and chital), Sloth and Himalayan Black bears, Indian Grey Mongoose, otters, yellow-throated martens, ghoral (goat-antelopes), Indian pangolins, and langur and rhesus monkeys. Owls and Nightjars can be heard during the night.

In the summer, elephants can be seen in herds of several hundred. The Indian python found in the reserve is a dangerous species, capable of killing a chital deer. Local crocodiles were saved from extinction by captive breeding programs that subsequently released crocodiles into the Ramganga river.

Ecotourism

Early-morning encounter with a Sambar deer in Jim Corbett National Park, on a guided elephant tour from the Dhikala tourist lodge.

Though the main focus is protection of wildlife, the reserve management has also encouraged ecotourism. In 1993, a training course covering natural history, visitor management and park interpretation was introduced to train nature guides. A second course followed in 1995 which recruited more guides for the same purpose. This allowed the staff of the reserve, previously preoccupied with guiding the visitors, to carry out management activities uninterrupted. Additionally, the Indian government has organized workshops on ecotourism in Corbett National Park and Garhwal region to ensure that the local citizens profit from tourism while the park remains protected.

Tiwari & Joshi (1997) consider summer (April-June) to be the best season for Indian tourists to visit the park while recommending the winter months (November-January) for foreign tourists. According to Riley & Riley (2005): "Best chances of seeing a tiger to come late in the dry season- April to mid June-and go out with mahouts and elephants for several days."

As early as 1991, the Corbett National Park played host to 3237 tourist vehicles carrying 45,215 visitors during the main tourist seasons between 15 November and 15 June. This heavy influx of tourists has led to visible stress signs on the natural ecosystem. Excessive trampling of soil due to tourist pressure has led to reduction in plant species and has also resulted in reduced soil moisture. The tourists have increasingly used fuel wood for cooking. This is a cause of concern as this fuel wood is obtained from the nearby forests, resulting in greater pressure on the forest ecosystem of the park. Additionally, tourists have also caused problems by making noise, littering and causing disturbances in general.

In 2007, young naturalist and photographer - Kahini Ghosh Mehta - took up the challenge of promoting healthy tourism in Corbett National Park and made the first comprehensive travel guide on Corbett. The film titled - Wild Saga of Corbett - showcases how tourists can contribute in their own small way in conservation efforts. The film is loaded with all information needed by a tourist before planning a visit to the park along with tips from senior park officials, nature guides and naturalists. Tourists can get a DVD copy of this film from the Bombay Natural History Society (BNHS).

A local N.G.O. named "RAINBOW FRIENDS OF NATURE & ENVIRONMENT" is working here for Nature & Wildlife Conservation for past 16 years. This organisation is a non-registered & self financed N.G.O. All its conservation activities are done with the self contribution of its own members. This N.G.O. works with school kids of Ramnagar town as well as from the surrounding villages.

Two of it's active members (Prashant Kumar & Gaurav Tiruwa) are also running a travel house at Corbett with the name of "EXP UTTARAKHAND travel solutions". Both of the guys are very sincere for what they are doing. Travelers who are going to visit Corbett National Park are strongly advised to contact these guys for at least once.

Other Attractions

Dhikala: This well-known destination in Corbett is situated at the fringes of Patli Dun valley. There is a rest house here which was built hundred of years ago. Kanda ridge forms the backdrop, and from Dhikala, one can enjoy the spectacular natural beauty of the valley.

Garjia Temple: It's located on the banks of river Kosi, nearly 14 km away from Ramnagar City. At the time of Kartik

Poornima, a fair is held here. The temple is dedicated to Garjia Devi.

Ranikhet: This is one of the beautiful hill station located in the Almora district of Uttaranchal. Tourists can view the eye catching views of Indian Himalayan from this place. This hill station receives heavy snow fall from December to February.

Elephant Safari: The ride on this majestic animal is one of the major attractions of Corbett National Park. Sitting on an elephant, like a royal, you go into the grasslands and jungles looking for tigers or a herd of wild elephants. Two times a day, Elephant safaris are arranged that starts from Dhikala-early morning and late afternoon.

Treks

Tourists are not allowed to have a walk inside the park, but they are allowed to go for trekking around the park, only with a guide. This place becomes very cold in the winter season, so tourists should make proper arrangements for themselves, if they are travelling in the winter season.

Kalagarh Dam: This dam is located in the south west direction of the Jim Corbett wildlife sanctuary. This is one of the best places for the bird watching tour. Lots of migratory waterfowl comes here in the winters.

Location

Corbett National Park is situated in Ramnagar in the district of Nainital, Uttaranchal.

Area: 521 km2

Route: The town of Ramnagar is the headquarters of Corbett Tiger Reserve. There are overnight trains available from Delhi to Ramnagar. Also, there are trains from Varanasi via Lucknow to Ramnagar. Reaching Ramnagar, one can hire a taxi to reach the park and Dhikala.

Ramnagar is also well connected by road with Lucknow, Nainital, Ranikhet, Haridwar, Dehradun and New Delhi. One can also drive from Delhi (295 km) via Gajraula, Moradabad, Kashipur to reach Ramnagar. A direct train to Ramnagar runs from New Delhi. Alternatively, one can come up to Haldwani/Kashipur/Kathgodam and come to Ramnagar by road.

Best Time to Visit: Mid-November to Mid-June.

An elephant herd at Jim Corbett National Park

A major incident in the history of the reserve followed the construction of a dam at the Kalagarh river and the submerging of 80 km2 (31 sq mi) of prime low lying riverine area. The consequences ranged from local extinction of swamp deer to a massive reduction in hog deer population. The reservoir formed due to the submerging of land has also led to an increase in aquatic fauna and has additionally served as a habitat for winter migrants.

Two villages situated on the southern boundary were shifted to the Firozpur-Manpur area situated on Ramnagar-Kashipur highway during 1990-93; the vacated areas were designated as buffer zones. The families in these villages were mostly dependent on forest products. With the passage of time, these areas began to show signs of ecological recovery. Vines, herbs, grasses and small trees began to appear, followed by herbaceous flora, eventually leading to natural forest type. It was observed that grass began to grow on the vacated agricultural fields and the adjoining forest areas started recuperating. By 1999-2002 several plant species emerged in these buffer zones. The newly arisen lush green fields attracted grass eating animals, mainly deer and elephants, who slowly migrated towards these areas and even preferred to stay there throughout the monsoon.

There were 109 cases of poaching recorded in 1988-89. This figure dropped to 12 reported cases in 1997-98 .

In 1985 David Hunt, a British ornithologist and birdwatching tour guide, was killed by a tiger in the park.

Present

The habitat of the reserve faces threats from invasive species such as the exotic weeds Lantana, Parthenium and Cassia. Natural resources like trees and grasses are exploited by the local population while encroachment of at least of 13.62 ha (0.05 sq mi) by 74 families has been recorded.

The villages surrounding the park are at least 15-20 years old and no new villages have come up in the recent past. The increasing population growth rate and the density of population within 1 km (0.62 mi) to 2 km (1.24 mi) from the park present a challenge to the management of the reserve. Incidents of killing cattle by tigers and leopards have led to acts of retaliation by the local population in some cases. The Indian government has approved the construction of a 12 km (7.5 mi) stone masonry wall on the southern boundary of the reserve where it comes in direct contact with agricultural fields.

In April, 2008, the National Conservation Tiger Authority (NCTA) expressed serious concern that protection systems have weakened, and poachers have infiltrated into this park. Monitoring of wild animals in the prescribed format has not been followed despite advisories and observations made during field visits. Also the monthly monitoring report of field evidence relating to tigers has not been received since 2006. NTCA said that in the "absence of ongoing monitoring protocol in a standardised manner, it would be impossible to forecast and keep track of untoward happenings in the area targeted by poachers." A cement road has been built through the park against a Supreme Court order. The road has become a thoroughfare between Kalagarh and Ramnagar. Constantly increasing vehicle traffic on this road is affecting the wildlife of crucial ranges like Jhirna, Kotirau and Dhara. Additionally, the Kalagarh irrigation colony that takes up about 5 square kilometers (1.9 sq mi) of the park is yet to be vacated despite a 2007 Supreme Court order

The Leopard of Rudraprayag was a male man-eating leopard, claimed to have killed over 125 people. It was eventually killed by famed big cat hunter and author Jim Corbett.

The first victim of the leopard was a villager of village Benji. For eight years, no one dared move alone at night on the road between the Hindu shrines of Kedarnath and Badrinath, for it passed through the leopard's territory, and few villagers would leave their houses. The leopard was apparently so desperate for food that it would break down doors, leap through windows, claw through the mud or thatch walls of huts and drag people from them, devouring them. The British Parliament requested the aid of Corbett in the autumn of 1925. In the town of Rudraprayag there is a sign-board which marks the spot where the leopard was shot. There is a fair held at Rudraprayag commemorating the killing of the leopard and people there often consider Jim Corbett a Sadhu.

Corbett's notes revealed that this leopard, an elderly male, was suffering from serious gum recession and tooth loss. Recent analysis of many of the man-eaters taken by Corbett and other hunters has shown a pattern, in which the animals are too sick or compromised to hunt their normal prey, and thus turn to hunting humans, who are much easier to hunt and kill than wild game.

Edward James "Jim" Corbett (25 July 1875 in Nainital, India - 19 April 1955 in Nyeri, Kenya) was a British hunter, conservationist and naturalist, famous for slaying a large number of man-eating tigers and leopards in India.

Corbett held the rank of colonel in the British Indian Army and was frequently called upon by the government of the United Provinces, now the Indian states of Uttar Pradesh and Uttarakhand, to slay man-eating tigers and leopards who had killed people in the villages of the Garhwal and Kumaon region. His success in slaying the man-eaters earned him much respect and fame amongst the people residing in the villages of Kumaon, many of whom considered him a sadhu (saint).

Corbett was an avid photographer and after his retirement, authored the Man-Eaters of Kumaon, Jungle Lore and other books recounting his hunts and experiences, which enjoyed much critical acclaim and commercial success. Corbett spoke out for the need to protect India's wildlife from extermination. The Corbett National Park in Kumaon was named in his honour in 1957.

Early life

Edward James Corbett was born of Irish ancestry in the town of Nainital near the Kumaon foothills of the Himalayas, in the United Provinces (now in the Indian state of Uttarakhand). Jim grew up in a large family of 13 children and was the eighth child of Christopher and Mary Jane Corbett. His parents had moved to Nainital in 1862, after Christopher Corbett had been appointed postmaster of the town. In winters, the family used to move to the foothills, where they owned a cottage near Kaladhungi, which was later known as Chhoti Haldwani or Corbett's Village. After his father's death, when Jim was 4 years old, his eldest brother Tom took over as the postmaster of Nainital. From a very young age, Jim was fascinated by the forests and the wildlife around his home in Kaladhungi. At a young age he learned to identify most animals and birds by their calls - owing to his frequent excursions. Over time he became a good tracker and hunter. Jim studied at the Oak Openings School, later renamed Philander Smith College, and St. Joseph's College in Nainital. Before he was 19, he quit school and found an employment with the Bengal and North Western Railway, initially working as a fuel inspector at Manakpur in the Punjab, and subsequently as a contractor for the trans-shipment of goods across the Ganges at Mokameh Ghat in Bihar.

Hunting man-eating Tigers

Between 1907 and 1938, Corbett tracked and shot a documented 19 tigers and 14 leopards-a total of 33 recorded and documented man-eaters. It is estimated that these big cats had killed more than 1,200 men, women and children. The first tiger he killed, the Champawat Tiger in Champawat, was responsible for 436 documented deaths.

He also shot the Panar Leopard, which allegedly killed 400 people after being injured by a poacher and thus being rendered unable to hunt its normal prey. Other notable man-eaters he killed were the Talla-Des man-eater, the Mohan man-eater, the Thak man-eater and the Chowgarh tigress. However, one of the most famous was the man-eating Leopard of Rudraprayag, which terrorised the pilgrims to the holy Hindu shrines Kedarnath and Badrinath for more than ten years.

This leopard's skull and dentition showed advanced, debilitating gum disease and tooth decay, such as would limit the animal in killing wild game and drive it towards man-eating. The Thak man-eating tigress, when skinned by Corbett, revealed two old gunshot wounds; one in her shoulder had become septic, and as Corbett suggested, could have been the reason for the tigress to have turned man-eater. Recent analysis of carcasses, skulls and preserved remains show that most of the man-eaters were suffering from disease or wounds like porcupine quills embedded deep in the skin or old gunshot wounds, which never healed. In the foreword of Man Eaters of Kumaon, Corbett writes,

"The wound that has caused a particular tiger to take to man-eating might be the result of a carelessly fired shot and failure to follow up and recover the wounded animal, or be the result of the tiger having lost his temper while killing a porcupine".

As the idea of killing tigers and other wild animals had been a fashionable 'sport' among the ruling British in India, it is no surprise that so many man-eaters suddenly made their presence during the 1900s.

By his own account, Corbett shot the wrong animal at least once, and greatly regretted the incident. In addition, man-eaters are quite capable of stalking the hunter. Therefore, Corbett preferred to hunt alone and on foot when pursuing dangerous game. He often hunted with a small dog named Robin, about whom he wrote much in his first book The Man-Eaters of Kumaon.

At times, Corbett took great personal risks to save the lives of others. Still remembered in India as a great preservationist, his memories command fond respect in the areas where he worked.

Hunter Turned Conservationist

Corbett bought his first camera in the late 1920s, and inspired by his friend F. W. Champion, started to record tigers on cine film . Although he had an intimate knowledge of the jungle, this was demanding to obtain good pictures, as the animals were exceedingly shy. As his admiration for tigers and leopards grew, he resolved never to shoot them unless they turned man-eater or posed a threat to cattle. He expressed regret at killing the Bachelor of Powalgarh.

Corbett was deeply concerned about the fate of tigers and their habitat . He lectured to groups of school children about natural heritage and the need to conserve forests and their wildlife; promoted the foundation of the Association for the Preservation of Game in the United Provinces and the All-India Conference for the Preservation of Wildlife. Together with F. W. Champion he played a key role in establishing India's first national park in the Kumaon Hills, the Hailey National Park, initially named after Lord Malcolm Hailey. The park was renamed in his honour in 1957.

Retiring in Kenya

After 1947, Corbett and his sister Maggie retired to Nyeri, Kenya, where he continued to write and sound the alarm about declining numbers of jungle cats and other wildlife. Jim Corbett was at the Tree Tops Hotel, a hut built on the branches of a giant ficus tree, when Princess Elizabeth stayed there on February 5-6, 1952, at the time of the death of her father, King George VI. Corbett wrote in the hotel's visitors' register:

For the first time in the history of the world, a young girl climbed into a tree one day a Princess, and after having what she described as her most thrilling experience, she climbed down from the tree the next day a Queen- God bless her.

Jim Corbett died of a heart attack a few days after he finished writing his sixth book Tree Tops, and was buried at St. Peter's Anglican Church in Nyeri.

The Champawat Tiger was a female Bengal Tiger shot in 1911 by Jim Corbett. She was allegedly responsible for 436 documented deaths in Nepal and the Kumaon area of India mostly during the 19th century.

After having killed over 200 people in Nepal she was driven by the Nepalese Army across the border into India, where she continued her activities in the Kumaon District. She was so bold that she roamed the roads outside villages, roaring and terrorizing the villagers and often trying to break into huts.

The tigress had made a kill (a 16 year old girl) the day she was bagged by Jim Corbett. A post-mortem on the tigress showed the upper and lower canine teeth on the right side of her mouth were broken; the upper one in half, the lower one right down to the bone. This was the result of a gunshot.

In Champawat town, near to the Chataar Bridge and on the way to Lohaghat, one can see a "cement board" marking the place where the tigress was finally brought down. However, the exact place where the tigress was killed by Jim Corbett is closer to the present location of the Hydroelectric powerhouse about 1 Km from the "cement board".

The details about the Champawat Tigress and how it was brought down can be found in the book titled Maneaters of Kumaon (1944) authored by Jim Corbett himself.

The Indomalaya ecozone is one of the eight ecozones that cover the planet's land surface. It extends across most of South and Southeast Asia and into the southern parts of East Asia.

Also called the Oriental Realm by biogeographers, Indomalaya extends from Afghanistan and Pakistan through the Indian subcontinent and Southeast Asia to lowland southern China, and through Indonesia as far as Java, Bali, and Borneo, east of which lies the Wallace line, the ecozone boundary named after Alfred Russel Wallace which separates Indomalaya from Australasia. Indomalaya also includes the Philippines, lowland Taiwan, and Japan's Ryukyu Islands.

Most of Indomalaya was originally covered by forest, mostly tropical and subtropical moist broadleaf forests, with tropical and subtropical dry broadleaf forests predominant in much of India and parts of Southeast Asia. The tropical moist forests of Indomalaya are dominated by trees of the dipterocarp family (Dipterocarpaceae).

LEGACY

Jim's home at Chhoti Haldwani, Kaladhungi has been converted into a museum. The 221 acres (0.89 km2; 0.345 sq mi) village, which he bought in 1915, still has his memories intact in the form of the Chaupal called meeting place, Moti House, which Corbett had built for his friend Moti Singh, and the Corbett Wall, an about 4.5 miles (7.2 km) long wall built around the village to protect crops from wild animals.

Jim Corbett's first book Man-eaters of Kumaon was a great success in India, the United Kingdom and the United States; the first edition of the American Book-of-the-Month Club being 250,000 copies and later translated into 27 languages. His 4th book Jungle Lore is considered his autobiography.

The Jim Corbett National Park in Uttarakhand, India has been renamed in his honour in 1957. He had played a key role in establishing this protected area in the 1930s.

In 1968, one of the five remaining subspecies of tigers was named after him: Panthera tigris corbetti, the Indochinese Tiger, also called Corbett's tiger.

In 1994 and 2002, the long-neglected graves of Corbett and his sister were repaired and restored by Jerry A. Jaleel, founder and director of the Jim Corbett Foundation.

Documentary

In 1986, the BBC produced a docudrama titled Man-Eaters of India with Fred Treves in the role of Jim Corbett. An IMAX movie India: Kingdom of the Tiger based on Corbett's books, was made in 2002 starring Christopher Heyerdahl as Jim Corbett. A TV movie based on The Man-Eating Leopard of Rudraprayag starring Jason Flemyng was made in 2005.

A trip from Kanyakumari to Thirparappu Waterfall is full of adventure and thrill. A journey to this picturesque spot near Kanyakumari is a memorable experience of a lifetime.

While traveling from Kanyakumari to Thirparappu Waterfall tourists can discover the beautiful places in and around the region like Vattakottai, Muttom beach, Gandhi mandap and Amman temple and many more.

The beautiful waterfall descending from Kodayar River is located at a distance of 60 km from Kanyakumari. After reaching Kanyakumari, there are a number of buses, auto rickshaws and taxis that connect people to different parts of the city. To reach Thirparappu Falls, the Trivandrum highway route through the village of Nagercoil can be accessed. The falls lies close to Kulasekhara village that was once ruled by kings.

Thirparappu Waterfall in Kanyakumari falls is 300 feet long and consists of a rocky riverbed. The view of the water, falling from a height of 50 feet, is truly magnificent. The Thirparappu weir has been built on the rocky mass that stretches far across the distance covering one fourth of a kilometer in the direction against the streams current. This weir supplies water to the fields that are used for irrigation.

A small temple dedicated to Lord Shiva is situated on the banks of the river. There are strong walls and fortifications that surround the temple. Recently, a swimming pool has been constructed nearby, so that children can enjoy their trip from Kanyakumari to Thirparappu Waterfall to the fullest.

Major Ecological Regions

The World Wildlife Fund (WWF) divides Indomalaya into three bioregions, which it defines as "geographic clusters of ecoregions that may span several habitat types, but have strong biogeographic affinities, particularly at taxonomic levels higher than the species level (genus, family)."

Indian Subcontinent

The Indian Subcontinent bioregion covers most of India, Pakistan, Bangladesh, Nepal, Bhutan, and Sri Lanka. The Hindu Kush, Karakoram, Himalaya, and Patkai ranges bound the bioregion on the northwest, north, and northeast; these ranges were formed by the collision of the northward-drifting Indian subcontinent with Asia beginning 45 million years ago. The Hindu Kush, Karakoram, and Himalaya are a major biogeographic boundary between the subtropical and tropical flora and fauna of the Indian subcontinent and the temperate-climate Palearctic ecozone.

Indochina

The Indochina bioregion includes most of mainland Southeast Asia, including Myanmar, Thailand, Laos, Vietnam, and Cambodia, as well as the subtropical forests of southern China.

Malesia is a botanical province which straddles the boundary between Indomalaya and Australasia. It includes the Malay Peninsula and the western Indonesian islands (known as Sundaland), the Philippines, the eastern Indonesian islands, and New Guinea. While the Malesia has much in common botanically, the portions east and west of the Wallace Line differ greatly in land animal species; Sundaland shares its fauna with mainland Asia, while terrestrial fauna on the islands east of the Wallace line are derived at least in part from species of Australian origin, such as marsupial mammals and ratite birds.

History

The flora of Indomalaya blends elements from the ancient supercontinents of Laurasia and Gondwana. Gondwanian elements were first introduced by India, which detached from Gondwana approximately 90 MYA, carrying its Gondwana-derived flora and fauna northward, which included cichlid fish and the flowering plant families Crypteroniaceae and possibly Dipterocarpaceae. India collided with Asia 30-45 MYA, and exchanged species. Later, as Australia-New Guinea drifted north, the collision of the Australian and Asian plates pushed up the islands of Wallacea, which were separated from one another by narrow straits, allowing a botanic exchange between Indomalaya and Australasia. Asian rainforest flora, including the dipterocarps, island-hopped across Wallacea to New Guinea, and several Gondwanian plant families, including podocarps and araucarias, moved westward from Australia-New Guinea into western Malesia and Southeast Asia.

Flora and Fauna

Two orders of mammals, the colugos (Dermoptera) and treeshrews (Scandentia), are endemic to the ecozone, as are families Craseonycteridae (Kitti's Hog-nosed Bat), Diatomyidae, Platacanthomyidae, Tarsiidae (tarsiers) and Hylobatidae (gibbons). Large mammals characteristic of Indomalaya include the leopard, tigers, water buffalos, Asian Elephant, Indian Rhinoceros, Javan Rhinoceros, Malayan Tapir, orangutans, and gibbons.

Indomalaya has three endemic bird families, the Irenidae (leafbirds and fairy bluebirds), Megalaimidae and Rhabdornithidae (Philippine creepers). Also characteristic are pheasants, pittas, Old World babblers, and flowerpeckers.

Indomalaya Terrestrial Ecoregions

Indomalaya Tropical and subtropical moist broadleaf forests

v o d o e

Andaman Islands rain forests

India

Borneo lowland rain forests

Brunei, Indonesia, Malaysia

Borneo montane rain forests

Brunei, Indonesia, Malaysia

Borneo peat swamp forests

Brunei, Indonesia, Malaysia

Brahmaputra Valley semi-evergreen forests

India

Cardamom Mountains rain forests

Cambodia, Thailand, Vietnam

Chao Phraya freshwater swamp forests

Thailand

Chao Phraya lowland moist deciduous forests

Thailand

Chin Hills-Arakan Yoma montane forests

Burma, India

Christmas and Cocos Islands tropical forests

Australia

Eastern highlands moist deciduous forests

India

Eastern Java-Bali montane rain forests

Indonesia

Eastern Java-Bali rain forests

Indonesia

Greater Negros-Panay rain forests

Philippines

Hainan Island monsoon rain forests

China

Himalayan subtropical broadleaf forests

Bhutan, India, Nepal

Irrawaddy freshwater swamp forests

Burma

Irrawaddy moist deciduous forests

Burma

Jian Nan subtropical evergreen forests

China

Kayah-Karen montane rain forests

Burma, Thailand

Lower Gangetic Plains moist deciduous forests

Bangladesh, India

Luang Prabang montane rain forests

Laos

Luzon montane rain forests

Philippines

Luzon rain forests

Philippines

Malabar Coast moist forests

India

Maldives-Lakshadweep-Chagos Archipelago tropical moist forests

British Indian Ocean Territory, India, Maldives

Meghalaya subtropical forests

India

Mentawai Islands rain forests

Indonesia

Mindanao montane rain forests

Philippines

Mindanao-Eastern Visayas rain forests

Philippines

Mindoro rain forests

Philippines

Mizoram-Manipur-Kachin rain forests

Bangladesh, India, Burma

Myanmar coastal rain forests

Burma

Nansei Islands subtropical evergreen forests

Japan

Nicobar Islands rain forests

India

North Western Ghats moist deciduous forests

India

North Western Ghats montane rain forests

India

Northern Annamites rain forests

Laos, Vietnam

Northern Indochina subtropical forests

China, Laos, Burma, Thailand, Vietnam

Northern Khorat Plateau moist deciduous forests

Laos, Thailand

Northern Thailand-Laos moist deciduous forests

Laos, Thailand

Northern Triangle subtropical forests

Burma

Northern Vietnam lowland rain forests

Vietnam

Orissa semi-evergreen forests

India

Palawan rain forests

Philippines

Peninsular Malaysian montane rain forests

Malaysia, Thailand

Peninsular Malaysian peat swamp forests

Malaysia, Thailand

Peninsular Malaysian rain forests

Indonesia, Malaysia

Red River freshwater swamp forests

Vietnam

South China Sea Islands

disputed between China, Malaysia, Philippines, Taiwan, Vietnam

South China-Vietnam subtropical evergreen forests

China, Vietnam

South Taiwan monsoon rain forests

Taiwan

South Western Ghats moist deciduous forests

India

South Western Ghats montane rain forests

India

Southern Annamites montane rain forests

Cambodia, Laos, Vietnam

Southwest Borneo freshwater swamp forests

Indonesia

Sri Lanka lowland rain forests

Sri Lanka

Sri Lanka montane rain forests

Sri Lanka

Sulu Archipelago rain forests

Philippines

Sumatran freshwater swamp forests

Indonesia

Sumatran lowland rain forests

Indonesia

Sumatran montane rain forests

Indonesia

Sumatran peat swamp forests

Indonesia

Sundaland heath forests

Indonesia

Sundarbans freshwater swamp forests

Bangladesh, India

Taiwan subtropical evergreen forests

Taiwan

Tenasserim-South Thailand semi-evergreen rain forests

Malaysia, Burma, Thailand

Tonle Sap freshwater swamp forests

Cambodia, Vietnam

Tonle Sap-Mekong peat swamp forests

Cambodia, Vietnam

Upper Gangetic Plains moist deciduous forests

India

Western Java montane rain forests

Indonesia

Western Java rain forests

Indonesia

Indomalaya Tropical and subtropical dry broadleaf forests

v o d o e

Central Deccan Plateau dry deciduous forests

India

Central Indochina dry forests

Cambodia, Laos, Thailand, Vietnam

Chota-Nagpur dry deciduous forests

India

East Deccan dry evergreen forests

India

Irrawaddy dry forests

Burma

Kathiarbar-Gir dry deciduous forests

India

Narmada Valley dry deciduous forests

India

Northern dry deciduous forests

India

South Deccan Plateau dry deciduous forests

India

Southeastern Indochina dry evergreen forests

Cambodia, Laos, Thailand

Southern Vietnam lowland dry forests

Vietnam

Sri Lanka dry-zone dry evergreen forests

Sri Lanka

Indomalaya Tropical and subtropical coniferous forests

v o d o e

Himalayan subtropical pine forests

Bhutan, India, Nepal, Pakistan

Luzon tropical pine forests

Philippines

Northeast India-Myanmar pine forests

Burma, India

Sumatran tropical pine forests

Indonesia

Indomalaya Temperate broadleaf and mixed forests

v o d o e

Eastern Himalayan broadleaf forests

Bhutan, India, Nepal

Northern Triangle temperate forests

Burma

Western Himalayan broadleaf forests

India, Nepal, Pakistan

Indomalaya Temperate coniferous forests

v o d o e

Eastern Himalayan subalpine conifer forests

Bhutan, India, Nepal

Western Himalayan subalpine conifer forests

India, Nepal, Pakistan

Indomalaya Tropical and subtropical grasslands, savannas, and shrublands

v o d o e

Terai-Duar savanna and grasslands

Bhutan, India, Nepal, Philippines

Indomalaya Flooded grasslands and savannas

v o d o e

Rann of Kutch seasonal salt marsh

India, Pakistan

Indomalaya Montane grasslands and shrublands

v o d o e

Kinabalu montane alpine meadows

Malaysia

Indomalaya Deserts and xeric shrublands

v o d o e

Deccan thorn scrub forests

India, Sri Lanka

Indus Valley desert

India, Pakistan

Northwestern thorn scrub forests

India, Pakistan

Thar desert

India, Pakistan

Indomalaya Mangrove

v o d o e

Godavari-Krishna mangroves

India

Indochina mangroves

Cambodia, Malaysia, Thailand, Vietnam

Indus River Delta-Arabian Sea mangroves

Pakistan

Myanmar coast mangroves

Burma, India, Malaysia, Thailand

Sunda Shelf mangroves

Brunei, Indonesia, Malaysia

Sundarbans mangroves

Bangladesh, India

Sangla is a scenic hill-town in the Baspa Valley, also referred to as the Sangla valley. The region is part of Kinnaur District in the Indian state of Himachal Pradesh. The valley is surrounded by richly forested slopes and offers delightful views of the high mountains. The Baspa hydel-project is also nearing completion, and the importance of the place is bound to increase.

Sangla valley was nominated as one of the five most beautiful valleys in the world by a reputed travel magazine. It is located in Kinnaur district of the Indian state ,Himachal Pradesh,very near to the Tibetan border. Its location in the greater Himalayan range gives it a climate which is boon to heat-weary plainspeople. Till 1989 outsiders could not enter the valley without a special permit from the Government of

India,due to its strategic position on the Indo-Tibet/China border.Sangla has managed to retain its pristine nature and is famous for pine nut orchards, Royal red apples and cherry trees, unspoilt glacial streams and quaint little villages like Chitkul, Karchham and Batseri which are just a few miles from Sangla.The Kinnauri people are famous for their distinct culture,their own dialect and simple but elegant lifestyles.The women are renowned for their beauty as also for their dominant position in the society. Apart from the stunning natural beauty of the place, the Himachal Pradesh government has also woken up to the adventure sport potential of the place and has been promoting trekking ,troutfishing.

Chapter-4

Hunting Wild Animals with Camera

Hunting is the practice of pursuing living animals (usually wildlife) for food, recreation, or trade. In present-day use, the term refers to lawful hunting, as distinguished from poaching, which is the killing, trapping or capture of the hunted species contrary to applicable law. The species which are hunted are referred to as game and are usually mammals and migratory or non-migratory gamebirds.

Hunting can also involve the elimination of vermin, as a means of pest control to prevent diseases caused by overpopulation. Hunting advocates state that hunting can be a necessary component of modern wildlife management, for example to help maintain a population of healthy animals within an environment's ecological carrying capacity when natural checks such as predators are absent. In the United States, wildlife managers are frequently part of hunting regulatory and licensing bodies, where they help to set rules on the number, manner and conditions in which game may be hunted.

The pursuit, capture and release, or capture for food of fish is called fishing, which is not commonly categorized as a form of hunting. Trapping is also usually considered a separate activity. Neither is it considered hunting to pursuc animals without intent to kill them, as in wildlife photography or birdwatching. The practice of hunting for plants or mushrooms is a colloquial term for foraging or gathering.

Skillful tracking and acquisition of an elusive target have caused the word hunting to be used in the vernacular as a metaphor, as in "bargain hunting" or "hunting down corruption and waste".

Hunting has a long history and may well pre-date the rise of species Homo sapiens. While our earliest Hominid ancestors were probably frugivore or omnivore, there is evidence that early Homo, and possibly already Australopithecine species have used larger animals for subsistence, and that hunting may have been one of the multiple environmental factors leading to replacement of holocene megafauna by smaller herbivores.

Of the closest surviving relatives of the human species, Pan, the Common Chimpanzee has an omnivorous diet including troop hunting behavior based on beta males led by an alpha male, while the less violent Bonobos, have a mostly frugivorous diet.

While it is undisputed that early humans were hunters, the importance of this fact for the final steps in the emergence of the Homo genus out of earlier Australopithecines, with its bipedalism and production of stone tools, and eventually also control of fire, are emphasized in the "hunting hypothesis", and de-emphasized in scenarios that stress the omnivore status of humans as their recipe for success, and social interaction, including mating behaviour as essential in the emergence of behavioral modernity.

With the establishment of language, culture and religion, hunting became a theme of stories and myths, besides rituals such as dance and animal sacrifice. Hunting was a crucial component of hunter-gatherer societies before the domestication of livestock and the dawn of agriculture, beginning about 11,000 years ago. By the Mesolithic, hunting strategies had diversified with the develop ent of the bow (by

18,000 years ago) and the domestication of the dog (about 15,000 years ago).

There is fossil evidence for spear use in Asian hunting dating from approximately 16,200 years ago. The North American megafauna extinction was coincidental with the Younger Dryas impact event, making hunting a less critical factor in prehistoric species loss than had been previously thought.

Many species of animals have been hunted and caribou/ wild reindeer "may well be the species of single greatest importance in the entire anthropological literature on hunting" (see also Reindeer Age).

Hunter-gathering lifestyles remained prevalent in the New World and Sub-Saharan Africa (with the notable exception of Aztec and Incan agriculture) until the European Age of Discovery, and they persist in some tribal societies, albeit in rapid decline. Peoples that preserved paleolithic hunting-gathering until the recent past include some indigenous peoples of the Amazonas (Aché), some Central and Southern African Bushmen (Hadza people, Khoisan), some peoples of New Guinea (Fayu), the Mlabri of Thailand and Laos, the Vedda people of Sri Lanka and a handful of uncontacted peoples.

Antiquity

Even as animal domestication became relatively widespread, hunting was usually a significant contributor to the human food supply, even after the development of agriculture. The supplementary meat and materials from hunting included protein, bone for implements, sinew for cordage, fur, feathers, rawhide and leather used in clothing. The earliest hunting tools would have included rocks, spears, the atlatl, bow and arrows.

On ancient reliefs, especially from Mesopotamia, kings are often depicted as hunters of big game such as lions, especially from a war chariot. The cultural and psychological importance of hunting in ancient societies is represented by deities such as the horned god Cernunnos, or lunar goddesses of classical antiquity, Greek Artemis or Roman Diana. Taboos are often related to hunting, and mythological association of prey species with a divinity could be reflected in hunting restrictions such as a 'reserve' surrounding a temple. Euripides' tale of Artemis and Actaeon, for example, may be seen as a caution against disrespect of prey or impudent boasting.

Hunting is still vital in marginal climates, especially those unsuited for pastoral uses or agriculture. Inuit peoples in the Arctic trap and hunt animals for clothing. From the skins of sea mammals, they may make kayaks, clothing, and footwear.

With domestication of the dog, birds of prey and the ferret, various forms of animal-aided hunting developed including venery (scent hound hunting, such as fox hunting), coursing (sight hound hunting), falconry and ferreting. These are all associated with medieval hunting; in time various dog breeds were selected for very precise tasks during the hunt, reflected in such names as pointer and setter.

Even as agriculture and animal husbandry became more prevalent, hunting often remained as a part of human culture where the environment and social conditions allowed. Hunting may be used to kill animals which prey upon domestic animals or to attempt to extirpate animals seen by humans as competition for resources such as water or forage.

As hunting moved from a subsistence activity to a social one, two trends emerged. One was that of the specialist hunter with special training and equipment. The other was the emergence of hunting as a sport for those of an upper social class. The meaning of the word "game" in middle English evolved to include an animal which is hunted.

As game became more of a luxury than a necessity, the stylized pursuit of it also became a luxury. Dangerous hunting, as for lions or wild boars, usually on horseback (or from a chariot) had a function similar to tournaments and manly sports. Hunting was considered to be an honourable, somewhat competitive pastime to help the aristocracy practice skills of war in times of peace.

In most parts of medieval Europe, the upper class obtained the sole rights to hunt in certain areas of a feudal territory. Game in these areas was certainly used as a source of food and furs, often provided via professional huntsmen; but it was also expected to provide a form of recreation for the aristocracy. The importance of this proprietary view of game can be seen in the Robin Hood legends, in which one of the primary charges against the outlaws is that they "hunt the King's deer". In the European medieval period, hunting was considered part of the set of seven mechanical arts.

Use of Dogs

Although various animals have been used to aid the hunter, none has been as important as the dog. The domestication of the dog has led to a symbiotic relationship in which the dog has lost its evolutionary independence from humans in exchange for support.

Dogs today are used to find, chase and retrieve game and sometimes to kill it. Hunting dogs allow humans to pursue and kill prey that would otherwise be very difficult or dangerous to hunt.

Indian and Eastern Religions

Hindu Scriptures describe hunting as an acceptable occupation as well as a sport of the kingly. Even figures considered godly are described to have engaged in hunting. One of the names of the god Shiva is "Mrigavyadha", the deer hunter ("mriga" means deer, "vyadha" means hunter). In the epic Ramayana, Dasharatha, the father of Rama, is said to have the ability to hunt in the dark. During one of his hunting expedition he accidentally killed Shravana, mistaking him for game. During Rama's exile in the forest, Ravana kidnapped his wife Sita from their hut while Rama was hunting a golden deer, and his brother Lakshman went after him. According to the Mahabharat, Pandu, the father of the Pandavas, accidentally killed the sage Kindama and his wife with an arrow mistaking them for a deer. Krishna is said to have died after being accidentally wounded by an arrow of a hunter.

Jainism teaches to have tremendous respect for all of life. Prohibitions for hunting and meat eating are the fundamental conditions for being a Jain.

The first Precept of Buddhism is the respect for all sentient life. The general approach by all Buddhists is to avoid killing any living animals. The Buddha explained the issue by saying "all fear death; comparing others with oneself, one should neither kill nor cause to kill".

From early Christian times, hunting has been forbidden to Roman Catholic Church clerics. Thus the "Corpus Juris Canonici" says "We forbid to all servants of God hunting and expeditions through the woods with hounds; and we also forbid them to keep hawks or falcons." The Fourth Council of the Lateran, held under Pope Innocent III, decreed "We interdict hunting or hawking to all clerics." The decree of the Council of Trent is worded more mildly: "Let clerics abstain from illicit hunting and hawking", which seems to imply that not all hunting is illicit, and canonists generally make a distinction declaring noisy (clamorosa) hunting unlawful but not quiet (quieta) hunting.

Ferraris gives it as the general sense of canonists that hunting is allowed to clerics if it be indulged in rarely and for sufficient cause, as necessity, utility or "honest" recreation, and with that moderation which is becoming to the ecclesiastical state. Ziegler, however, thinks that the interpretation of the canonists is not in accordance with the letter or spirit of the laws of the Church.

Nevertheless, although a distinction between lawful and unlawful hunting is undoubtedly permissible, it is certain that a bishop can absolutely prohibit all hunting to the clerics of his diocese, as was done by synods at Milan, Avignon, Liège, Cologne and elsewhere. Benedict XIV declared that such synodal decrees are not too severe, as an absolute prohibition of hunting is more conformable to the ecclesiastical law. In practice, therefore, the synodal statutes of various localities must be consulted to discover whether they allow quiet hunting or prohibit it altogether.

It is important to note that the Bible places no such restrictions on any Christian, as most do not observe Kosher dietary laws. Hence Protestant clerics, Catholic lay parishioners, and Protestants have no religious restrictions on hunting. This is in accord with what is found in the Bible book of Acts 15:28-29 and 1 Timothy 4:4.

Jewish hunting law, based on the Torah, is similar, permitting hunting of non-preying animals that are additionally considered Kosher for food, although hunting preying animals for food is strictly prohibited under Rabbinic law. Hence birds of prey are specifically prohibited and non-Kosher. Hunting for sport, and not for food is also forbidden in Rabbinical Law.

Hunting Culture

New Zealand

New Zealand has a strong hunting culture. The islands making up New Zealand originally had no land mammals apart from bats. However, once Europeans arrived game animals were introduced by acclimatisation societies to provide New Zealanders with sport and a hunting resource. Deer, pigs, goats, rabbits, Tahr and Chamois all adapted well to the New Zealand terrain and with no natural predators their population exploded. Government agencies view the animals as pests due to their effects on the natural environment and on agricultural production, but hunters view them as a resource.

Shikar (India)

During the feudal and colonial epoch on the Indian continent, hunting was a true 'regal sport' in the numerous princely states, as many (Maha)rajas, Nawabs, as well as British officers maintained a whole corps of shikaris, who were native professional hunters. They would be headed by a master of the hunt, who might be styled Mir-shikar. Often these were recruited from the normally low-ranking local tribes because of their traditional knowledge of environment and hunting techniques. Big game, such as Bengal tigers, might be hunted from the back of an elephant.

Indian social norms are generally antagonistic to hunting, while a few sects like the Bishnoi lay special emphasis on the conservation of particular species like the antelope. India's Wildlife Protection Act of 1972 bans the killing of all wild animals. However, the Chief Wildlife Warden may, if he is satisfied that any wild animal from a specified list has become dangerous to human life or is so disabled or diseased as to be beyond recovery, permit any person to hunt such animal. In such a case, the body of any wild animal killed or wounded becomes government property.

Safari: Distinct Way of Hunting

A safari, from a Swahili word meaning a long journey, is an overland journey (especially in Africa).

Safari as a distinctive way of hunting was popularized by US author Ernest Hemingway and president Theodore Roosevelt. A safari may consist of several days or even weeks-long journey and camping in the bush or jungle, while pursuing big game. Nowadays, it's often used to describe tours through African national parks to watch or hunt wildlife.

Hunters are usually tourists, accompanied by (licensed and highly regulated) professional hunters ("PH"), local guides, skinners and porters in more difficult terrains. A special safari type is the solo-safari where all the license acquiring, stalking, preparation and outfitting is done by the hunter himself.

Photo-safaris were popular even before the advent of ecotourism. The synonym "bloodless hunt" for hunting with the use of film and a still photo camera was first used by the Polish photographer W?odzimierz Puchalski.

United Kingdom

Fox hunting is the type of hunting most closely associated with the United Kingdom. Originally a form of vermin control to protect livestock, it became a popular social activity for newly wealthy upper classes in Victorian times, and a traditional rural activity for riders and foot followers alike. Similar to fox hunting in many ways is the chasing of hare with hounds. Sight hounds such as greyhounds may be used to run down hare in coursing with scent hounds such as beagles. Other sorts of foxhounds may also be used for hunting deer or mink. Hunting deer on foot using stealth without hounds or horses is called deer stalking.

These forms of hunting have been controversial in the UK. Animal welfare supporters believe that hunting causes unnecessary suffering to foxes, horses and hounds. Proponents argue that it is culturally and perhaps economically important. Using dogs to chase wild mammals was made illegal in February 2005 by the Hunting Act 2004. The issues involved are addressed in the article fox hunting legislation.

Shooting Traditions

The shooting of game birds, especially pheasants still exists in the UK, with the British Association for Shooting and

Conservation saying that over a million people per year participate in shooting, although this figure includes game shooting, clay pigeon shooting and target shooting. Shooting, as opposed to traditional hunting, requires little questing for game - around 35 million birds are released onto shooting estates every year, some having been factory farmed. Shoots can be elaborate affairs with guns placed in assigned positions with assistants to help load shotguns. When in position, "beaters" move through the areas of cover swinging sticks or flags to drive the game out. Such events are often called "drives". The open season for grouse in the UK begins on August 12, the so-called Glorious Twelfth. The definition of game in the United Kingdom is governed by the Game Act 1831.

United States

North American hunting predates the United States by thousands of years, and was an important part of many pre-Columbian Native American cultures. Native Americans retain some hunting rights and are exempt from some laws as part of Indian treaties and otherwise under federal law-examples include eagle feather laws and exemptions in the Marine Mammal Protection Act. This is considered particularly important in Alaska Native communities.

Regulation of hunting is primarily regulated by state law; additional regulations are imposed through United States environmental law in the case of migratory birds and endangered species.

Regulations vary widely from state to state, and govern the areas, time periods, techniques and methods by which specific game animals may be hunted. Some states make a distinction between protected species and unprotected species (often vermin or varmints) for which there are no hunting regulations. Hunters of protected species require a hunting license in all states, for which completion of a hunting safety course is sometimes a prerequisite.

Typically game animals are divided into several categories for regulatory purposes. Typical categories, along with example species, are as follows:

- Big game: white-tailed deer, mule deer, moose, elk, caribou, bighorn sheep, pronghorn, boar, javelina
- Small Game: rabbit, hare, squirrel, oppossum, raccoon, porcupine, skunk, ring-tailed cat, armadillo
- Furbearers: beaver, red fox, mink, pine martin, musk rat, otter, bobcat
- Predators: cougar (mountain lion/panther), bear, coyote
- Upland game bird: grouse, turkey, chukar, pheasant, quail, dove
- Waterfowl: duck, teal, merganser, geese, swan

Hunting big game typically requires a "tag" for each animal harvested. Tags must be purchased in addition to the hunting license, and the number of tags issued to an individual is typically limited. In cases where there are more prospective hunters than the quota for that species, tags are usually assigned by lottery. Tags may be further restricted to a specific area or "wildlife management unit." Hunting migratory waterfowl requires a "duck stamp" from the Fish and Wildlife Service.

Harvest of animals other than big game is typically restricted by a "bag limit" and a "possession limit." A bag limit is a maximum number of a specific animal species that an individual can harvest in a single day. A possession limit is a maximum number of a specific animal species that can be in an individual's possession at any time.

Guns usage in hunting is also typically regulated by game category, area within the state, and time period. Regulations for big game hunting often specify a minimum caliber or muzzle energy for firearms. The use of rifles is often banned for safety reasons in areas with high population density or limited topographic relief. Regulations may also limit or ban the use of lead in ammunition because of environmental concerns. Specific seasons for bow hunting or muzzle-loading black powder guns are often established to limit competition with hunters using more effective weapons. Hunting in the United States is not associated with any particular class or culture. In fact, 78% of Americans support legal hunting, but relatively few Americans actually hunt. At the beginning of the 21st century, 6% of Americans hunted. Southerners in states along the eastern seaboard hunted at a rate slightly below the national average (5%), and while hunting was more common in other parts of the South (9%), these rates did not surpass those of the Plains states, where 12% of Midwesterners hunted. Hunting in other areas of the country fell below the national average. Overall in the 1996-2006 period, the number of hunters over the age of 16 declined by 10%, a drop attributable to a number of factors including habitat loss and changes in recreation habits.

Regulation of hunting within the United States dates from the 19th century. Some modern hunters see themselves as conservationists and sportsmen in the mode of Theodore Roosevelt and the Boone and Crockett Club. Local hunting clubs and national organizations provide hunter education and help protect the future of the sport by buying land for future hunting use. Some groups represent a specific hunting interest, such as Ducks Unlimited, Pheasants Forever or Delta Waterfowl Foundation. Many hunting groups also participate in lobbying the federal government and state government.

Each year, nearly $200 million in hunters' federal excise taxes are distributed to state agencies to support wildlife management programs, the purchase of lands open to hunters, and hunter education and safety classes. Since 1934 the sale of Federal Duck Stamps, a required purchase for migratory waterfowl hunters over 16 years old, has raised over $700 million to help purchase more than 5.2 million acres (8,100 sq mi/20,000 km^2) of habitat for the National Wildlife Refuge System lands that support waterfowl and many other wildlife species, and are often open to hunting. States also collect monies from hunting licenses to assist with management of game animals, as designated by law. A key task of Federal and state park rangers and game wardens is to enforce laws and regulations related to hunting, including species protection, hunting seasons, and hunting bans.

Varmint hunting is an American phrase for the selective killing of non-game animals seen as pests. While not always an efficient form of pest control, varmint hunting achieves selective control of pests while providing recreation and is much less regulated. Varmint species are often responsible for detrimental effects on crops, livestock, landscaping, infrastructure, and pets. Some animals (such as wild rabbits or squirrels) may be utilized for fur or meat, but often no use is made of the carcass. Which species are "varmints" depends on the circumstance and area. Common varmints may include various rodents, coyotes, crows, foxes, feral cats, and feral hogs. Some animals once considered varmints are now protected, such as wolves. In the US state of Louisiana, a non-native rodent known as a nutria have become so destructive to the local ecosystem that the state has initiated a bounty program to help control the population. Feral dogs and cats, rats, starlings, English sparrows, and pigeons may be hunted without a hunting license in the United States.

Fair Chase

The principles of the Fair Chase have been a part of the American hunting tradition for over 100 years. The role of the hunter-conservationist, popularized by Theodore Roosevelt, has been central to the development of the modern Fair Chase tradition. When internet hunting was introduced in 2005, allowing people to hunt over the internet using remotely controlled guns, the practice was widely criticized by hunters as violating the principles of fair chase. As a representative of the NRA explained, "he NRA has always maintained that fair chase, being in the field with your firearm or bow, is an important element of hunting tradition. Sitting at your desk in front of your computer, clicking at a mouse, has nothing to do with hunting."

Wildlife Management

Hunting gives resource managers an important tool in managing populations that might exceed the carrying capacity of their habitat and threaten the well-being of other species or, in some instances, damage human health or safety. Hunting reduces intraspecific competition for food and shelter, reducing mortality among the remaining animals. Some environmentalists assert that (re)introducing predators would achieve the same end with greater efficiency and less negative effect such as introducing significant amounts of free lead into the environment and food chain. Hunters often disagree, arguing that hunting is more selective, removing fewer old, sick, or young animals than natural predation. Aldo Leopold, an early environmentalist and hunter, also believed hunting could be used to manage animal populations.

Management agencies sometimes rely on hunting to control specific animal populations, as has been the case with deer in North America. These hunts may sometimes be carried out by professional shooters although others may include amateur hunters. Many U.S. city and local governments hire professional and amateur hunters each year to reduce populations of animals that are becoming hazardous, like deer, in a restricted area, such as neighborhood parks and metropolitan open spaces.

A large part of managing populations involves managing the number and, sometimes, the size or age of animals harvested so as to ensure the sustainability of the population. Tools which are frequently used to control harvest are bag limits and season closures, although gear restrictions such as archery-only seasons are becoming increasingly popular in an effort to reduce hunter success rates.

Bag Limits

Bag limits are provisions under the law which control how many animals of a given species or group of species can be killed although there are often species for which bag limits do not apply. There are also jurisdictions where bag limits are not applied at all or are not applied under certain circumstances. Where bag limits are used, however, there can be daily or seasonal bag limits. For example, ducks can often be harvested at a rate of six per hunter per day. Big game, like moose, most often have a seasonal bag limit of one animal per hunter. Bag limits may also regulate the size, sex or age of animal that a hunter can kill. In many cases, bag limits are designed to more equitably allocate harvest among the hunting population rather than to protect animal populations. The phrase "bag limits" comes from the custom among hunters of small game to carry successful kills in a small bag, similar to a fishing kreel.

Closed Season

A closed season is a "hunting" term used to describe a time during which hunting an animal of a given species is contrary to law. Typically, closed seasons are designed to protect a species when they are most vulnerable or, sometimes, to protect them during their breeding season . By extension, the period that is not the closed season is known as the open season.

Laws

Illegal hunting and harvesting of wild species contrary to local and international conservation and wildlife management laws is termed as "Poaching". Violations of hunting laws and regulations are normally punishable by law and, collectively, such violations are known as poaching.

Methods

Historical, subsistence and sport hunting techniques can differ radically, with modern hunting regulations often addressing issues of where, when and how hunts are conducted. Techniques may vary depending on government regulations, a hunter's personal ethics, local custom, hunting-equipment and the animal being hunted. Often a hunter will use a combination of more than one technique. Laws may forbid sport hunters from using some methods used primarily in poaching and wildlife management.

- Baiting is the use of decoys, lures, scent.
- Battue involves beating animals into a killing-zone or ambush
- Beagling is the use of beagles in hunting rabbits and sometimes in hunting foxes
- Beating uses beaters to flush out game and/or drive it into position
- Blind or stand hunting is waiting for animals from a concealed or elevated position
- Calling is the use of animal noises to attract or drive animals
- Camouflage is the use of visual concealment (or scent) to blend with the environment
- Dogs may be used to course or to help flush, herd, drive, track, point at, pursue or retrieve prey
- Driving is the herding of animals in a particular direction, usually toward another hunter in the group
- Flushing is the practice of scaring animals from concealed areas
- Glassing is the use of optics (such as binoculars) to more easily locate animals
- Glue is an indiscriminate passive form to kill birds

- Internet hunting is a method of hunting over the internet using webcams and remotely controlled guns
- Netting, including active netting with the use of cannon nets and rocket nets
- Persistence hunting is the use of running and tracking to pursue the prey to exhaustion.
- Scouting includes a variety of tasks and techniques for finding animals to hunt
- Spotlighting or shining is the use of artificial light to find or blind animals before killing
- Stalking or still hunting is the practice of walking quietly, in search of animals or in pursuit of an individual animal
- Tracking is the practice of reading physical evidence in pursuing animals
- Trapping is the use of devices (snares, pits, deadfalls) to capture or kill an animal

What is Trophy Hunting?

Trophy hunting is the selective seeking of wild game. It may also include the controversial hunting of captive or semi-captive animals expressly bred and raised under controlled or semi-controlled conditions so as to attain trophy characteristics (canned hunts).

In the 19th century, southern and central European sport hunters often pursued game only for a trophy, usually the head or pelt of an animal, which was then displayed as a sign of prowess. The rest of the animal was typically discarded. Some cultures, however, disapprove of such waste. In Nordic countries, hunting for trophies was-and still is-frowned upon. Hunting in North America in the 19th century was done primarily as a way to supplement food supplies, although it is now undertaken mainly for sport . The safari method of hunting was a development of sport hunting that saw elaborate travel in Africa, India and other places in pursuit of trophies. In modern times, trophy hunting persists and is a significant industry in some areas.

Trophy hunting is most often criticized when it involves rare or endangered animals. Opponents may also see trophy hunting as an issue of morality or animal cruelty, criticising the killing of living creatures for recreation. Victorian era dramatist W. S. Gilbert remarked, "Deer-stalking would be a very fine sport if only the deer had guns."

There is also debate about the extent to which trophy hunting benefits the local economy. Hunters argue that fees paid contribute to the local economy and provide value to animals that would otherwise be seen as competition for grazing, livestock, and crops. This analysis is disputed by opponents of trophy hunting. Some argue that the animals are worth more to the community for ecotourism, than hunting.

Eco-tourism and Safari Hunter

A variety of industries benefit from hunting and support hunting on economic grounds. In Tanzania, it is estimated that a safari hunter spends 50-100 times that of the average eco-tourist. The average photo tourist may demand luxury accommodations. In contrast, the average safari hunter stays in tented camps. Safari hunters are also more likely to use remote areas, uninviting to the average eco-tourist. Advocates argue that these hunters allow for anti-poaching activities and revenue for local communities. In the United Kingdom, the game hunting of birds as an industry is said[who?] to be extremely important to the rural economy: The Cobham Report of 1997 suggested it to be worth around £700 million, and hunting and shooting lobby groups now claim it to be worth over a billion.

Hunting also has a significant financial impact in the United States, with many companies specializing in hunting equipment or specialty tourism. Today's hunters come from a broad range of economic, social, and cultural backgrounds. In 2001, over 13 million hunters averaged eighteen days hunting and spent over $20.5 billion on their sport. In the U.S., proceeds from hunting licenses contribute to state game management programs including preservation of wildlife habitat.

Hunters have been driving forces throughout history in the movement to ensure long-term sustainability of natural resources and wildlife habitats. Some hunters feel that the honor once bestowed upon their sport has diminished over the years, claiming that mainstream media sometimes ignores the connection between hunting and conservation and often publishes claims that hunting endangers wildlife. Of greater concern to endangered wildlife is the loss of habitat, brought on by overpopulation and urban development. Because of their connection with the land and vested interest in increasing wildlife populations, hunters have been influential in implementing and financing various programs geared towards habitat restoration and conservation. Hunters have worked closely with local and federal governments to enact legislation to protect wildlife habitats. The following examples represent hunter-advocated legislation enacted to generate funds for preserving and establishing habitats.(Hunters Rule). The Ontario Federation of Anglers and Hunters successfully lobbied to prevent cuts in funding for the Community Fisheries and Wildlife Involvement Program by 50%.

In 1937, hunters successfully lobbied Congress to pass the Pittman-Robertson Wildlife Restoration Act, which placed an 11% tax on all hunting equipment. This self-imposed tax now generates over $700 million each year and is used exclusively to establish, restore and protect wildlife habitats. It is named for Nevada Senator Key Pittman and Virginia Congressman Absalom Willis Robertson.

On March 16, 1934 President Roosevelt signed the Migratory Bird Hunting Stamp Act, which requires an annual stamp purchase by all hunters over the age of sixteen. The stamps are created on behalf of the program by the U.S. Postal Service and depict wildlife artwork chosen through an annual contest. They play an important role in habitat conservation because 98% of all funds generated by their sale go directly toward the purchase or lease of wetland habitat for protection in the National Wildlife Refuge System. In addition to waterfowl, it is estimated that one third of the nation's endangered species seek food and shelter in areas protected using Duck Stamp funds. Since 1934, the sale of Federal Duck Stamps has generated $670M and helped to purchase or lease 5.2 million acres (21,000 km²) of habitat. The stamps serve as a license to hunt migratory birds, an entrance pass for all National Wildlife Refuge areas and are also considered collectors items often purchased for aesthetic reasons outside of the hunting and birding communities. Although non-hunters buy a significant number of Duck Stamps, 87% of their sales are contributed to hunters. Distribution of funds is managed by The Migratory Bird Conservation Commission (MBCC).

Many photographers, be them amateur or professional, find pleasure in capturing animals on film. If you have taken photography as a hobby then you may want to learn the basics of animal photography as well. The good thing about taking photos of animals is that the basic requirements are universal, whether you are planning to photograph the tiniest insects or the largest land animals.

One very important thing to remember when shooting animals is to always put safety above all other considerations. It doesn't matter if you are shooting a domestic or a wild animal, you should always ensure both your safety and that of the animal. Camera flashes and shutter noises can frighten even the tamest animal, and even domestic animals can be dangerous when they are frightened. Remember not to get too close, especially if you are taking photos of wild animals. This poses a danger to you because the animal may attack, and it poses a risk for the animal as well because most wild animals tend to abandon their natural habitat when they are bothered too much.

You should approach animal photography in the same way that you approach human portraiture. This is not to say that you should make the animal pose for the picture like a human, but that you should measure lighting and composition in much the same way as you do in shooting a human portrait. Watch the position of the animal's body, locate the shadows, and check the composition just as you normally would with a human subject.

In animal photography, making sure that the animal's eyes are in sharp focus is very effective in creating maximum impact. This is because the eyes are the primary means by which human beings connect with other species. Even in animals, the eyes can be windows to the soul as they are able to convey strong emotion and intelligence. When you are shooting a partial body portrait of any animal, use the rule of thirds and position the eyes at a good intersection point. You would also do well to take note that among the most breathtaking animal shots are those that catch them in the middle of an activity or show them while interacting with their surroundings.

It is very important to fill the frame in animal photography, except in cases where you want the landscape to be as much of a subject as the animal. Many animals are very small in stature, so they will need to be very large in the frame in order to create a good shot. But, of course, just like in action photography, you have to make sure that there is enough room between the animal's face and the edge of the frame. And be very careful in choosing your background. Litter and man-made structures can ruin an animal photo. Your most powerful weapon in these cases is the use of a shallow depth of field.

Why Photograph Wildlife?

Nature has been one of the primary subjects of photography for over 115 years. The natural beauty that surrounds us in the form of landscapes, plants, and wildlife is a compelling subject to capture in still images.

But more than that, the experience of taking photography of wildlife is one of the most thrilling forms of the craft. There is something deeply compelling-almost primeval-about sharing a wooded glen with wild animals, gaining their trust, and documenting their beauty and behavior.

Wildlife is not the easiest subject to capture. It often requires larger, telephoto lenses, or if your interests lie in the tiny, macro lenses that allow for magnification and close focusing. Wildlife is most active at dawn and dusk-time when light is not always cooperative. Fast telephoto lenses are an option if you have a nice line of credit available, but they're not always necessary. Today's manufacturers have some more affordable, slower telephotos that can be used to capture great wildlife images.

Getting Close and Keeping Steady

Animals are inherently more sensitive to the shape and form of an upright human being than they are to vehicles. You can attribute this to the thousands of years we've spent hunting them for food. The fear that animals have for humans is well deserved. Many wildlife photographers use expensive and complicated blinds to hide their presence from animals. In the right circumstances though, you already have a working blind-your vehicle.

Some more cautious animals will flee at the sight of a vehicle. Kestrels, for instance, flee at the sight of a car as much as they do a human being. But many species feel much more comfortable around them than they do people, especially in national parks where vehicles are a common sight, such as Rocky Mountain National Park or Yellowstone. I can't tell you how many times I've been able to get remarkably close to elk in Rocky Mountain National Park.

Unfortunately too often, a tourist with a point-and-shoot camera comes along and steps out of their vehicle and approaches the animals. The elk shy away or bolt into the trees, and my shoot is over.

Stabilizing your camera inside a car isn't often easy. You can set up some tripods so that you can shoot from the driver or passenger seat, but some wildlife photographers find the tripod too constrictive, especially when photographing animals on the move.

In those situations, your window is your friend. Roll up your window to the level at which you want to set your lens. Buy some cheap pipe insulation with a slit down one side at any hardware store. Slip this over the edge of the glass of your window and you can comfortably rest your lens on the edge. I have seen photographers use bean bags for the same purpose.

Remember the rule of thumb to eliminate camera shake: you should be shooting at a shutter speed at or above the effective focal length of your lens. That means if you shoot like I do with a 70-300mm lens on an Olympus body with a 2x sensor crop factor, you need a shutter speed of at least 1/600th of a second to help ensure that your image will be as sharp as it can be.

Tripods and the window edge trick can help lower this shutter speed, as well as cameras or lenses with image stabilization. The kind of blur we're talking about isn't always obvious when you check an image with your LCD. With this rule of thumb, you help reduce the chances of being disappointed with what you thought were great shots in the field, but turned out to be blurry or soft when loaded onto your computer. Don't be afraid to increase your ISO to get the shutter speeds you need. When shooting fast-moving animals such as birds in flight, you may want a shutter speed as high as 1/1000th of a second to freeze your subject. And of course, proper technique in stabilizing your camera can go a long way.

Most photographer recommend that you use at least a 300mm (35mm equivalent) telephoto for wildlife photography. Any less and you will have difficulty filling the frame with your subject. But no matter how much reach your longest lens gives you, you'll always be left wanting more. Teleconverters can be used, at the cost of sharpness and f-stops, but for bird photography involving small subjects, they may be your best option.

Practice Your Skills

Before spending a fortune on a photography expedition to Africa, hone your skills in your own backyard. My area of Colorado is rife with red-winged blackbirds in the spring. They can be found around nearly any body of water, and the males are claiming and protecting territory from nearly every tree branch or cattail. Their focus on competitors and attracting a mate means that their guard is down more than it would be at other times, and the cattails they often frequent are conveniently located at eye level.

I have found that red-winged blackbirds are an excellent "practice subject" to work on my skills of approach, framing, and general technical work (exposure, focus, and the general fiddling of knobs and buttons). They are common enough that if you blow an approach by moving too quickly or loudly, another will most likely present itself shortly. But they are not so easy to catch. Dark subjects against light backgrounds can be a technical challenge, and learning to expose the blacks of their feathers along with that red patch can really hone your skills.

Blackbirds may not be common in your area, but most likely, some form of wildlife frequents the parks and fields in your area. Find a good "practice subject" and work on your basics, so that when you go after bigger, more impressive animals, you will have a solid foundation in the basic techniques and you will stand a better chance of capturing a great image.

Know Your Subject

Get to know your subject's behavior. Read books and talk with hunters or experts on the species. Your local university may have researchers who special in the animal you're trying to capture. Politely ask them for tips via email-often they will be more than happy to share their expertise, provided you're respectful of the animals.

Some knowledge you will only gain through experience. I've spent most of the winter travelling to Rocky Mountain National Park on a weekly basis. Of particular interest in this park are the herds of wild elk. A large bachelor herd is my favorite subject, but finding them in time for the good light was not easy at first. Over time, and through trial and error, I began to understand how weather affected which altitudes the animals could be found at. Colder weather or snow would push them down into lower elevations where it they were easier to find and photograph. Also, I learned which park entrances they were most likely to be near at the time of day I was photographing them. Other photographers in your area may be able to share this information, but I think if you can spare the time, it's more fulfilling to learn their behavior on your own.

Speaking of parks, the local rangers and park staff are an excellent resource for learning the activities and whereabouts of great subjects. I often swing into the pay station later in the morning to chat with the rangers about how things have been inside the park. As amateur photographers, we're not able to spend all of our time out there, but the rangers do, and they excellent resources at your disposal.

Capture Action!

Starting out, I was content to capture any animal in focus, properly exposed, and decently composed. I didn't care so much what they were doing in the image, so long as I got them in the shot and they weren't just a speck in the distance. As you develop your other skills, however, you will find that the most compelling and successful images are one that capture an animal in action. It's common sense, but often, we forget in the excitement of just being near the animal that that closeness is not easily conveyed through still photography.

Capturing action requires more patience than just getting the animals in the frame. It's nearly impossible to approach an animal without impacting its behavior somewhat. They will often be rattled or cautious in your presence. It takes time for the animal to settle back into its routine, to forget that you're watching.

Increase your chances of capturing hunting or feeding behavior by photographing at dawn and dusk. The golden hour is great not just for light but for locating wildlife as well. Many animals are nocturnal or at the least crepuscular, so they are on the move at these times. Being out half an hour before sunrise or an hour before sunset will help ensure that you find your subjects when they're doing something more interesting than chewing their cud.

One last tip for capturing action with birds of prey was recently shared with me by wildlife photographer Vic Schendel. In his years of wildlife photography, he's discovered that raptors often defecate shortly before taking flight. When you have the bird in your frame, and you see this happen, starting firing off shots, because you are likely to catch a much more impressive image of the bird taking flight than if you had taken a shot while it rested on a tree branch or telephone wire.

Chapter-5

ENJOYING ADVENTUROUS SPORTS IN THE LAP OF NATURE

An extreme sport (also called action sport and adventure sport) is a popular term for certain activities perceived as having a high level of inherent danger, and that are counter-cultural. These activities often involve speed, height, a high level of physical exertion, and highly specialized gear or spectacular stunts.

The definition of an extreme sport is not exact - for example, although studies show that (road) cycling ranks as the sport with the highest rate of injury, it is not considered an extreme sport because it is not counter-cultural. The term's origin is also unclear, but it gained popularity in the 1990s when it was picked up by marketing companies to promote the X Games.

While use of the term "extreme sport" has spread far and wide to describe a multitude of different activities, exactly which sports are considered 'extreme' is debatable. There are however several characteristics common to most extreme sports. While not the exclusive domain of youth, extreme sports tend to have a younger-than-average target demographic. Extreme sports are rarely sanctioned by schools. Extreme sports tend to be more solitary than traditional sports. In addition, beginning extreme athletes tend to work on their craft without the guidance of a coach (though some may hire a coach later).

Activities categorized by media as extreme sports differ from traditional sports due to the higher number of inherently uncontrollable variables. Athletes in these activities compete not only against other athletes, but also against environmental obstacles and challenges. These environmental variables are frequently weather and terrain related, including wind, snow, water and mountains. Because these natural phenomena cannot be controlled, they inevitably affect the outcome of the given activity or event.

In a traditional sporting event, athletes compete against each other under controlled circumstances. While it is possible to create a controlled sporting event such as X Games, there are often variables that cannot be held constant for all athletes. Examples include snow conditions for snowboarders, rock and ice quality for climbers, and wave height and shape for surfers.

Whilst traditional sporting judgment criteria may be adopted when assessing performance (distance, time, score, et cetera), extreme sports performers are often evaluated on more subjective and aesthetic criteria. This results in a tendency to reject unified judging methods, with different sports employing their own ideals and indeed having the ability to evolve their assessment standards with new trends or developments in the sport.

Classification

In 2004, author Joe Tomlinson classified extreme sports into those that take place in air, land, and water,

Nine air sports are mentioned including: BASE jumping, bungee jumping, gliding, hang gliding, high wire, ski jumping, sky diving, sky surfing, and sky flying.

Eighteen land sports including:indoor climbing, adventure racing, aggressive inline skating, BMX, caving, extreme motocross, extreme skiing, freestyle skiing, land and ice yachting, mountain biking, mountain boarding, outdoor climbing, sandboarding, skateboarding, snowboarding, snowmobiling, speed biking, speed skiing, scootering and street luge.

Fifteen water sports including: barefoot water skiing, cliff diving, free-diving, jet skiing, open water swimming, powerboat racing, round the world yacht racing, scuba diving, snorkeling, speed sailing, surfing, wakeboarding, whitewater kayaking, windsurfing.

History

This section requires expansion.

The origin of the divergence of the term "extreme sports" from "sports" may date to the 1950s in the appearance of a phrase usually, but wrongly, attributed to Ernest Hemingway. The phrase is

"There are only three sports: bullfighting, motor racing, and mountaineering; all the rest are merely games."

The implication of the phrase was that the word "sport" defined an activity in which one might be killed. The other activities being termed "games". The phrase may have been invented by either writer Barnaby Conrad or automotive author Ken Purdy.

In recent decades the term extreme sport was further promoted by X Games, a multi-sport event created and developed by ESPN. The first X Games (known as 1995 Extreme Games) were held in Newport, Providence, Mount Snow, and Vermont in the United States.

A history of the sports was published in 2004. Amped: How Big Air, Big Dollars and a New Generation Took Sports to the Extreme. The book provided an overview of the history, culture, and business of the sports and included interviews with athletes, company owners, and marketers.

Marketing

Hang Glider Launching from Mount Tamalpais

Some contend, that the distinction between an extreme sport and a conventional one has as much to do with marketing as it has to do with perceptions about levels of danger involved or the amount of adrenaline generated. Furthermore a sport like rugby union, though dangerous and adrenaline-inducing, would not fall into the category of extreme sports due to its traditional image, and it does not have certain things that other extreme sports do, such as high speed and an intention to perform stunts. Demolition derby racing, predominantly an adult sport, is not usually thought of as 'extreme' while BMX racing, a youth sport, is.

In addition to the generational divide, one true hallmark of an extreme sport is a counter-cultural aura-a rejection of authority and the status quo by disaffected youth. The youth of Generation Y have seized upon activities which they can claim as their own, and have begun rejecting more traditional sports in increasing numbers.

Wingsuit flying is a recent activity.

The definition of extreme sports may have shifted over the years due to marketing trends. When the term first surfaced circa the late 1980s/early 1990s, it was used for adult sports such as skydiving, scuba diving, surfing, rock climbing, snow skiing, water skiing, snowboarding, mountain biking, mountaineering, storm chasing, hang gliding, and bungee jumping, many of which were undergoing an unprecedented growth in popularity at the time. Outside magazine, not the X Games, epitomized the meaning of the term, and if there was a clothing style associated with extreme sports it was an "outdoorsy" look favoring brand names associated with mountaineering or backpacking such as The North Face and Patagonia, Teva sandals or hiking boots for footwear, etc. The term nowadays applies more to youth sports like skateboarding, snowboarding, aggressive skating, FMX and BMX and is closely associated with marketing efforts aimed at the younger generation (e.g. the ad campaigns of Mountain Dew), and with their favored styles of clothing and music, especially the kind of urban baggy look associated with skateboarders, and loud, fast alternative rock. This shift in styles may also be partly a generational shift, as Baby Boomers and Generation X have aged and marketing efforts associated with extreme sports shifted toward the younger Generation Y demographic sometime in the mid to late 1990s.

The term gained popularity with the advent of the X Games, a made-for-television collection of events. Advertisers were quick to recognize the appeal of the event to the public, and as a consequence competitors and organizers are not wanting for sponsorship. The high profile of extreme sports and the culture surrounding them has also led to parodies such as Extreme ironing, urban housework, extreme croquet, and house gymnastics.

Adrenaline rush

Snowboarder drops off a cornice.

A feature of such activities in the view of some is their alleged capacity to induce an adrenaline rush in participants. However, the medical view is that the rush or high associated with the activity is not due to adrenaline being released as a response to fear, but due to increased levels of dopamine, endorphins and serotonin because of the high level of physical exertion. Furthermore, a recent study suggests that the link to adrenaline and 'true' extreme sports is tentative. The study defined 'true' extreme sports as a leisure or recreation activity where the most likely outcome of a mismanaged accident or mistake was death. This definition was designed to separate the marketing hype from the activity. Another characteristic of activities so labeled is they tend to be individual rather than team sports. Extreme sports can include both competitive and non-competitive activities.

Motivation

Eric Brymer also found that the potential of various extraordinary human experiences, many of which parallel those found in activities such as meditation, was an important part of the extreme sport experience.

Some of the sports have existed for decades and their proponents span generations, some going on to become well known personalities. Rock climbing and ice climbing have spawned publicly recognizable names such as Edmund Hillary, Chris Bonington, Wolfgang Gullich and more recently Joe Simpson. Another example is surfing, invented centuries ago by the inhabitants of Hawaii.

Bungee Jumping

Bungee jumping (also spelled "Bungy" jumping) is an activity that involves jumping from a tall structure while connected to a large elastic cord. The tall structure is usually a fixed object, such as a building, bridge or crane; but it is also possible to jump from a movable object, such as a hot-air-balloon or helicopter, that has the ability to hover above the ground. The thrill comes as much from the free-falling as from the rebounds.

When the person jumps, the cord stretches and the jumper flies upwards again as the cord snaps back, and continues to oscillate up and down until all the energy is dissipated.

The word "bungee" originates from West Country dialect, meaning "Anything thick and squat", as defined by James Jennings in his book "Observations of Some of the Dialects in The West of England" published 1825. Around 1930 the name became used for a rubber eraser. The word bungy, as used by A J Hackett, is "Kiwi slang for an Elastic Strap". Cloth-covered rubber cords with hooks on the ends have been available for decades under the generic name bungy cords.

In the 1950s David Attenborough and a BBC film crew brought back footage of the "land divers" (known as "Naghol") of Pentecost Island in Vanuatu, young men who jumped from tall wooden platforms with vines tied to their ankles as a test of their courage and passage into manhood. A similar practice, only with a much slower pace for falling, has been practised as the Danza de los Voladores de Papantla or the 'Papantla flyers' of central Mexico, a tradition dating back to the days of the Aztecs.

A tower 4,000 feet high with a system to drop a "car" suspended by a cable of "best rubber" was proposed for the Chicago World Fair, 1892-1893. The car, seating two hundred people, would be shoved from a platform on the tower and then bounce to a stop. The designer engineer suggested that for safety the ground below "be covered with eight feet of feather bedding". The proposal was declined by the Fair's organizers.

The first modern bungee jumps were made on 1 April 1979 from the 250-foot Clifton Suspension Bridge in Bristol, by David Kirke, Chris Baker, Simon Keeling, Tim Hunt and Alan Weston of the Oxford University Dangerous Sports Club. The jumpers were arrested shortly after, but continued with jumps in the US from the Golden Gate and Royal Gorge bridges, (this last jump sponsored by and televised on the American program That's Incredible) spreading the concept worldwide. By 1982 they were jumping from mobile cranes and hot air balloons.

Commercial bungee jumping began with the New Zealander, A J Hackett, who made his first jump from Auckland's Greenhithe Bridge in 1986. During the following years Hackett performed a number of jumps from bridges and other structures (including the Eiffel Tower), building public interest in the sport, and opening the world's first permanent commercial bungee site; the Kawarau Bridge Bungy at Queenstown in the South Island of New Zealand. Hackett remains one of the largest commercial operators, with concerns in several countries.

Despite the inherent danger of jumping from a great height, several million successful jumps have taken place since 1980. This is attributable to bungee operators rigorously conforming to standards and guidelines governing jumps, such as double checking calculations and fittings for every jump. As with any sport, injuries can still occur (see below), and there have been fatalities. A relatively common mistake in fatality cases is to use a cord that is too long. The cord should be substantially shorter than the height of the jumping platform to allow it room to stretch. When the cord reaches its natural length the jumper either starts to slow down or keeps accelerating depending upon the speed of descent. One may not even start to slow until the cord has been stretched a significant amount, because the cord's resistance to distortion is zero at the natural length, and increases only gradually after, taking some time to even equal the jumper's weight. See also Potential energy for a discussion of the spring constant and the force required to distort bungee cords and other spring-like objects.

Equipment

The elastic rope first used in bungee jumping, and still used by many commercial operators, is factory-produced braided shock cord. This consists of many latex strands enclosed in a tough outer cover. The outer cover may be applied when the latex is pre-stressed, so that the cord's resistance to extension is already significant at the cord's natural length. This gives a harder, sharper bounce. The braided cover also provides significant durability benefits. Other operators, including A J Hackett and most southern-hemisphere operators, use unbraided cords in which the latex strands are exposed (pictured at right). These give a softer, longer bounce and can be home-produced.

Although there is a certain elegance in using only a simple ankle attachment, accidents in which participants became detached led many commercial operators to use a body harness, if only as a backup for an ankle attachment. Body harnesses are generally derived from climbing equipment rather than parachute equipment.

Retrieval methods vary according to the site used. Mobile cranes provide the greatest recovery speed and flexibility, the jumper being lowered rapidly to ground level and detached. Many other mechanisms have been devised according to the nature of the jump platform and the need for a rapid turn-around.

The Highest Jump

In August 2005, AJ Hackett added a SkyJump to the Macau Tower, making it the world's highest jump at 233 metres (764 ft). The SkyJump did not qualify as the world's highest bungee as it is not strictly speaking a bungee jump, but instead what is referred to as a 'Decelerator-Descent' jump, using a steel cable and decelerator system, rather than an elastic rope. On 17 December 2006, The Macau Tower started operating a proper bungee jump, which became the "Highest Commercial Bungee Jump In The World" according to the Guinness Book of Records. The Macau Tower Bungy does have a "Guide cable" system which limits swing (the jump is very close to the structure of the tower itself) but does not have any effect on the speed of descent, so this still qualifies the jump for the World Record.

There is another commercial bungee jump currently in operation which is just 13m smaller, at 220 metres (720 ft). This jump, which is made without guide ropes, is located near Locarno, Switzerland and takes place from the top of the

Verzasca Dam. This jump was prominently featured in the opening scene of the James Bond film GoldenEye.

The Bloukrans Bridge in South Africa and the Verzasca Dam jumps are pure freefall swinging bungee from a single cord.

Bloukrans Bridge was opened in 1997 and uses a pendulum bungee system. It is 216m high, from the platform to the river below.

Guinness only records jumps from fixed objects to guarantee the accuracy of the measurement. John Kockleman however recorded a 2,200-foot (670 m) bungee jump from a hot air balloon in California in 1989. In 1991 Andrew Salisbury jumped from 9,000 feet (2,700 m) from a helicopter over Cancun for a television program and with Reebok sponsorship. The full stretch was recorded at 3,157 feet (962 m). He landed safely under parachute.

One commercial jump higher than all others is at the Royal Gorge Bridge in Colorado. The height of the platform is 321 metres (1,053 ft). However, this jump is rarely available, as part of the Royal Gorge Go Fast Games-first in 2005, then again in 2007.

In Popular Culture

Several major movies have featured bungee jumps, most famously the opening sequence of the 1995 James Bond film GoldenEye in which Bond makes a jump over the edge of a dam in Russia (in reality the dam is in Switzerland: Verzasca Dam, and the jump was genuine, not an animated special effect).

It appears in the title of the South Korean film Bungee Jumping of Their Own (Beonjijeompeureul hada 2001), although it does not play a large part in the film.

In 1986, the BBC TV program The Late, Late Breakfast Show, presented by Noel Edmonds, was taken off the air after a volunteer for its 'Whirly Wheel' live stunt section, Michael Lush, was killed while rehearsing a bungee jump.

In the 1982 Judge Dredd story "Criminal Heights", published in the Daily Star, bungee jumping was portrayed as the next 'craze' to catch on in the City.

A fictional proto-bungee jump is a plot point in the Michael Chabon novel The Amazing Adventures of Kavalier and Clay.

In the film Selena, in which Jennifer Lopez played Selena Quintanilla-Perez, she is shown bungee jumping at a carnival. This is an actual event which took place shortly before Selena's death in 1995.

Variations

Catapult

In "Catapult" (Reverse Bungee or Bungee Rocket) the 'jumper' starts on the ground. The jumper is secured and the cord stretched, then released and shooting the jumper up into the air. This is often achieved using either a crane or a hoist attached to a (semi-)perma structure. This simplifies the action of stretching the cord and later lowering the participant to the ground.

"Twin Tower" is similar with two oblique cords.

Trampoline

Bungy Trampoline uses, as its name suggests, elements from bungy and trampolining. The participant begins on a trampoline and is fitted into a body harness, which is attached via bungy cords to two high poles on either side of the trampoline. As they begin to jump, the bungy cords are tightened, allowing a higher jump than could normally be made from a trampoline alone.

Running

Bungee Running involves no jumping as such. It merely consists of, as the name suggests, running along a track (often inflatable) with a bungee cord attached. One often has a velcro-backed marker which is used to mark how far the runner got before the bungee cord pulled back. This activity can often be found at fairs, carnivals & is often most popular with children.

Ramp

Bungee jumping off a ramp. Two rubber cords - the "bungees" - are tied around the participants waist to a harness. Those bungee cords are linked to steel cables along which they can slide thanks to stainless pulleys. The participants ride bike, sled or ski before jumping. Thierry Devaux performs during his bungee jumps an aesthetical and creative move akin to dance or skating. . He performs 8 to 12 acrobatic figures during two-hour training with the help of his Jumar or with a winch to lift him up . He is also the inventor of a more ethical technique by directly using his elastic cord to climb up. . He stopped counting his jumps after the thousandth one, after sixteen years of training. He did six figures from the Eiffel Tower , nine figures for the Olympic Games , six figures from the Golden Gate Bridge and eight figures from the Brooklyn Bridge . After four attempts, he missed his three acrobatic jumps when he was landing on the torch of Statue of Liberty

Suspended Catch Air Device

SCAD diving is similar to bungee jumping in that participant is dropped from a height, but in this variation there is no cord, instead the participant falls into a net

Safety and Possible Injury

There is a wide spectrum of possible injuries during a jump. One can be injured during a jump if the safety harness fails, the cord elasticity is miscalculated, or the cord is not properly connected to the jump platform. In most cases this is a result of human error in the form of mishandled harness preparation. Another major injury is if the jumper experiences cord entanglement with their own body. Other injuries include eye trauma, rope burn, uterine prolapse, dislocations, bruises, whiplash, pinched fingers and back injury.

Age, equipment, experience, location and weight are some of the factors, and nervousness can exacerbate eye traumas.

In 1997, Laura Patterson, one of a 16-member professional bungee jumping team, died of massive cranial trauma when she jumped from the top level of the Louisiana Superdome with improperly handled bungee cords and collided head-first into the concrete-based playing field. She was practising for an exhibition intended to be performed during the halftime show of Super Bowl XXXI. The bungee jumping portion of the show was removed from the program and a commemoration of Patterson was added.

Hiking is an outdoor activity which consists of walking in natural environments, often on hiking trails. It is such a popular activity that there are numerous hiking organizations worldwide. The health benefits of different types of hiking have been confirmed in studies. The word hiking is understood in all English-speaking countries, but there are differences in usage.

In the United States and United Kingdom, hiking refers to cross-country walking of a longer duration than a simple walk and usually over terrain where hiking boots are required. A day hike refers to a hike that can be completed in a single day, often applied to mountain hikes to a lake or summit, but not requiring an overnight camp, in which case the term backpacking is used. Bushwhacking specifically refers to difficult walking through dense forest, undergrowth, or bushes, where forward progress requires pushing vegetation aside. In extreme cases of bushwhacking where the vegetation is so dense that human passage is impeded, a machete is used to clear a pathway. Australians use the term bushwalking for both on- and off-trail hiking. New Zealanders use tramping (particularly for overnight and longer trips), walking or bushwalking. Multi-day hiking in the mountainous regions of India, Nepal, North America, South America, and in the highlands of East Africa is also called trekking; the Dutch refer to trekking also. Hiking a long-distance trail from end-to-end is also referred to as trekking and as thru-hiking in some places, for example on the Appalachian Trail (AT) or Long Trail (LT) in Vermont. The Long Trail is the oldest long-distance hiking trail in the United States.

Comparison with Other Forms of Touring

Hiking is one of the fundamental outdoor activities on which many others are based. Many beautiful places can only be reached overland by hiking, and enthusiasts regard hiking as the best way to see nature. Hikers see it as better than a tour in a vehicle of any kind (or on an animal; see horseback riding) because the hiker's senses are not intruded upon by distractions such as windows, engine noise, airborne dust and fellow passengers. Hiking over long distances or over difficult terrain requires both the physical ability to do the hike and the knowledge of the route and its pitfalls.

Environmental Impact

Hikers often seek beautiful natural environments in which to hike. These environments are often fragile: hikers may accidentally destroy the environment that they enjoy. While the action of an individual may not strongly affect the environment, the mass effect of a large number of hikers can degrade the environment. For example, gathering wood in an alpine area to start a fire may be harmless if done once (except for wildfire risk). Years of gathering wood, however, can strip an alpine area of valuable nutrients. Generally, protected areas such as parks have regulations in place to protect the environment. If hikers follow such regulations, their impact can be minimized. Such regulations include forbidding wood fires, restricting camping to established camp sites, disposing or packing out faecal matter, imposing a quota on the number of hikers per mile.

Many hikers espouse the philosophy of Leave No Trace: hiking in a way such that future hikers cannot detect the presence of previous hikers. Practitioners of this philosophy obey its strictures, even in the absence of area regulations. Followers of this practice follow strict practices on dealing with food waste, food packaging, and alterations to the surrounding environment.

Human waste is often a major source of environmental impact from hiking. These wastes can contaminate the watershed and make other hikers ill. Bacterial contamination can be avoided by digging 'catholes' 10 to 25 cm (4 to 10 inches) deep, depending on local soil composition and covering after use. If these catholes are dug at least 60 m (200 feet) away from water sources and trails, the risk of contamination is minimized. Many hikers warn other hikers about the location of their catholes by marking them with sticks stuck into the ground.

Protecting the trails and nature areas can be taken further with the idea of taking out more than you brought in. If every responsible hiker took out one small bag of garbage left by others our trails and nature areas would gradually become pristine.

Sometimes hikers enjoy viewing rare or endangered species. However, some species (such as martens or bighorn sheep) are very sensitive to the presence of humans, especially around mating season. To prevent adverse impact, hikers should learn the habits and habitats of endangered species.

There is one situation where an individual hiker can make a large impact on an ecosystem: inadvertently starting a wildfire. For example, in 2005, a Czech backpacker burned 7% of Torres del Paine National Park in Chile by knocking over an illegal gas portable stove. Obeying area regulations and setting up cooking devices on designated areas (or if necessary on bare ground) will reduce the risk of wildfire.

Hazards

Hiking may produce threats to personal safety. These threats can be dangerous circumstances while hiking and/or specific accidents or ailments. Diarrhea has been found to be one of the most common illness afflicting long-distance hikers in the United States . (See Wilderness acquired diarrhea.)

Dangerous hiking circumstances include losing the way, inclement weather, hazardous terrain, or exacerbation of pre-existing medical conditions. Specific accidents include metabolic imbalances (such as dehydration or hypothermia), topical injuries (such as frostbite or sunburn), attacks by animals, or internal injuries (such as ankle sprain).

Hikers often propose a set of behavioral prescriptions to minimize these threats. A well-known example of such a set of prescription is the Ten Essentials.

Attacks by humans are also a reality. There are organizations that promote prevention, self defense and escape. The cell phone and GPS devices are used in some organizations.

In various countries, borders may be poorly marked. It is good practice to know where international borders are. Many nations, such as Finland, have specific rules governing hiking across borders.

Paragliding is a recreational and competitive flying sport. A paraglider is a free-flying, foot-launched aircraft. The pilot sits in a harness suspended below a fabric wing, whose shape is formed by its suspension lines and the pressure of air entering vents in the front of the wing.

In 1952 Domina Jalbert advanced governable gliding parachutes with multi-cells and controls for lateral glide.

In 1954, Walter Neumark predicted (in an article in Flight magazine) a time when a glider pilot would be "able to launch himself by running over the edge of a cliff or down a slope ... whether on a rock-climbing holiday in Skye or ski-ing in the Alps".

In 1961, the French engineer Pierre Lemoigne produced improved parachute designs which led to the Para-Commander. The 'PC', had cut-outs at the rear and sides that enabled it to be towed into the air and steered - leading to parasailing/ parascending.

Sometimes credited with the greatest development in parachutes since Leonardo da Vinci[by whom?], the American Domina Jalbert invented the Parafoil which had sectioned cells in an aerofoil shape; an open leading edge and a closed trailing edge, inflated by passage through the air - the ram-air design. He filed US Patent 3131894 on January 10, 1963.

Meanwhile, David Barish was developing the Sail Wing for recovery of NASA space capsules - "slope soaring was a way of testing out ... the Sail Wing". After tests on Hunter Mountain, New York in September 1965, he went on to promote 'slope soaring' as a summer activity for ski resorts (apparently without great success). NASA originated the term 'paraglider' in the early 1960s, and 'paragliding' was first used in the early 1970s to describe foot-launching of gliding parachutes.

In 1971, Steve Snyder marketing the first wing : Paraplane.

Author Walter Neumark wrote Operating Procedures for Ascending Parachutes, and he and a group of enthusiasts with a passion for tow-launching 'PCs' and ram-air parachutes eventually broke away from the British Parachute Association to form the British Association of Parascending Clubs (BAPC) in 1973. Authors Patrick Gilligan (Canada) and Betrand Dubuis (Switzerland) wrote the first flight manual "The Paragliding Manual" in 1985, officially coining the word Paragliding.

These threads were pulled together in June 1978 by three friends Jean-Claude Bétemps, André Bohn and Gérard Bosson from Mieussy Haute-Savoie, France. After inspiration from an article on 'slope soaring' in the Parachute Manual magazine by parachutist & publisher Dan Poynter, they calculated that on a suitable slope, a 'square' ram-air parachute could be inflated by running down the slope; Bétemps launched from Pointe du Pertuiset, Mieussy, and flew 100 m. Bohn followed him and glided down to the football pitch in the valley 1000 metres below. 'Parapente' (pente being French for slope) was born.

From the 1980s equipment has continued to improve and the number of paragliding pilots has continued to increase. The first World Championship was held in Kössen, Austria in 1989.

Equipment

Wing

The paraglider wing or canopy is known in aeronautical engineering as a ram-air airfoil, or parafoil. Such wings comprise two layers of fabric which are connected to internal supporting material in such a way as to form a row of cells. By leaving most of the cells open only at the leading edge, incoming air (ram-air pressure) keeps the wing inflated, thus maintaining its shape. When inflated, the wing's cross-section has the typical teardrop aerofoil shape.

In some modern paragliders (from the 1990s onwards), especially higher performance wings, some of the cells of the leading edge are closed to form a cleaner aerodynamic airfoil. Like the wingtips, these cells are kept inflated by the internal pressure of the wing Wings Infos.

The pilot is supported underneath the wing by a network of lines. The lines are gathered into two sets as left and right risers. The risers collect the lines in rows from front to back in either 3 or 4 rows, distributing load as in a whippletree. The risers are connected to the pilot's harness by two carabiners.

Paraglider wings typically have an area of 20-35 square metres (220-380 sq ft) with a span of 8-12 metres (26-39 ft), and weigh 3-7 kilograms (6.6-15 lb). Combined weight of wing, harness, reserve, instruments, helmet, etc. is around 12-18 kilograms (26-40 lb).

The glide ratio of paragliders ranges from 8:1 for recreational wings, to about 11:1 for modern competition models . For comparison, a typical skydiving parachute will achieve about 3:1 glide. A hang glider will achieve about 15:1 glide. An idling (gliding) Cessna 152 will achieve 9:1. Some sailplanes can achieve a glide ratio of up to 72:1.

The speed range of paragliders is typically 20-60 kilometres per hour (12-37 mph), from stall speed to maximum speed. Beginner wings will be in the lower part of this range, high-performance wings in the upper part of the range. The range for safe flying will be somewhat smaller.

Modern paraglider wings are made of high-performance non-porous fabrics such as OLKS from Gelvenor, with Dyneema/ Spectra or Kevlar/Aramid lines.

For storage and carrying, the wing is usually folded into a stuffsack (bag), which can then be stowed in a large backpack along with the harness. For pilots who may not want the added weight or fuss of a backpack, some modern harnesses include the ability to turn the harness inside out such that it becomes a backpack.

Tandem paragliders, designed to carry the pilot and one passenger, are larger but otherwise similar. They usually fly faster with higher trim speeds, are more resistant to collapse, and have a slightly higher sink rate compared to solo paragliders.

Since 2000 Juan Salvadori in Argentina has been exploring a variant wing termed Paramontante that involves some firm beams. In April 2009 Pere Casellas has joined in a collaboration with Juan Salvadori for polishing the paramontante. Laboratori d'envol Paramontante

Harness

The pilot is loosely and comfortably buckled into a harness which offers support in both the standing and sitting positions. Modern harnesses are designed to be as comfortable as a lounge chair in the sitting position. Many harnesses even have an adjustable 'lumbar support'. A reserve parachute is also typically connected to a paragliding harness.

The primary purpose of parachutes (including skydiving canopies) is for descending, as when jumping out of an aircraft or dropping cargo. In contrast, the primary purpose of paragliders is for ascending. Paragliders are categorized as "ascending parachutes" by canopy manufacturers worldwide, and are designed for "free flying" meaning flight without a tether (for an example of tethered flight, see parasailing). However, in areas without high launch points, paragliders may be towed aloft by a ground vehicle or a stationary winch, after which they are released, creating much the same effect as a mountain launch. Such tethered launches can give a paraglider pilot a higher starting point than many mountains do, offering similar opportunities to catch thermals and to remain airborne by "thermaling" and other forms of lift. As with other forms of free flight, paragliding requires the significant skill and training required for aircraft control, including aeronautical theory, meteorological knowledge and forecasting, personal/emotional safety considerations, adherence to applicable Federal Aviation Regulations (US), and knowledge of equipment care and maintenance.

INSTRUMENTS

Most pilots use variometers, radios, and, increasingly, GPS units when flying.

Variometer

Birds are highly sensitive to atmospheric pressure, and can tell when they are in rising or sinking air. People can sense the acceleration when they first hit a thermal, but cannot detect the difference between constant rising air and constant sinking air, so turn to technology to help. Modern variometers are capable of detecting rates of climb or sink of 1 cm per second, such is the case of the Flymaster B1 which uses extremely low noise electronics and complex algorithms to detect such minute changes in air pressure.

A variometer indicates climb-rate (or sink-rate) with short audio signals (beeps, which increase in pitch and tempo during ascent, and a droning sound, which gets deeper as the rate of descent increases) and/or a visual display. It also shows altitude: either above takeoff, above sea level, or (at higher altitudes) "flight level".

The main purpose of a variometer is in helping a pilot find and stay in the "core" of a thermal to maximise height gain and, conversely, to indicate when a pilot is in sinking air and needs to find rising air.

The more advanced variometers have an integrated GPS. This is not only more convenient, but also allows one to record the flight in three dimensions. The track of the flight is digitally signed and stored and can be downloaded after the landing. Digitally signed tracks can be used as proof for record claims, replacing the 'old' method of photo documentation.

Radios used are PTT (push-to-talk) transceivers, normally operating in or around the FM VHF 2-metre band (144-148 MHz). The "2 Meter" band is an amateur radio band, sometimes used for interpersonal communications, and Aviation Frequencies are usually 108 MHz to 136 MHz. Usually a microphone is incorporated in the helmet, and the PTT switch is either fixed to the outside of the helmet, or strapped to a finger.

Use of an Amateur Radio without a Federal Amateur Radio License is HIGHLY ILLEGAL!!!! Modifying said radio is also ILLEGAL! Fines will be issued WHEN you are caught. At least $15,000, but higher have also been issued upto $70,000, plus federal prison time. Radios are type accepted by the federal government according to the intended service. 150 Mhz to 170 Mhz is NOT for use on an Amateur Radio. A number of pilots use FRS/GMRS radios for pilot to pilot communications. There are other parts of the country where VHF radio contact is preferred, especially when flying out of local airports where regulations permit. Also, many pilots carry a cell phone so they can call for pickup should they land away from their point of destination.

VHF Aviation Band radios such as the Icom IC-A5, A6 or A23 are recommended. No license is required for their use. It is always good to be able to communicate with airports and other flyers, especially in the more populated parts of the country. In some areas, the ability to communicate with the control tower is required.

Use of radios made for the amateur 2 meter band is NOT legal unless you are a licensed amateur radio operator. Hams are very protective of their frequencies and do not like interference generated by unlicensed flyers. Many hams own direction finding equipment and will enjoy the sport of finding you and reporting you to the FCC. Recently, a major fly-in was issued a warning by the FCC not to use the 2 meter band for communciations. Also one California interferer was just sentenced to 7 years in jail and fined $25,000 for unlicensed use of 2 meters.

Unlicensed flyers are relatively easy to spot as they are not aware of the 2 meter band plan and will just "pick a frequency" for use. They stick out like a sore thumb and are easy to track.

Your best bet is to stick with FRS and aviation band radios.

GPS

GPS (global positioning system) is a necessary accessory when flying competitions, where it has to be demonstrated that way-points have been correctly passed.

It can also be interesting to view a GPS track of a flight when back on the ground, to analyze flying technique. Computer software is available which allows various different analyses of GPS tracks (e.g. CompeGPS, See You).

Other uses include being able to determine drift due to the prevailing wind when flying at altitude, providing position information to allow restricted airspace to be avoided, and identifying one's location for retrieval teams after landing-out in unfamiliar territory.

More recently, the use of GPS data, linked to a computer, has enabled pilots to share 3D tracks of their flights on Google Earth. This fascinating insight allows comparisons between competing pilots to be made in a detailed 'post-flight' analysis.

Control

Brakes: Controls held in each of the pilot's hands connect to the trailing edge of the left and right sides of the wing. These controls are called 'brakes' and provide the primary and most general means of control in a paraglider. The brakes are used to adjust speed, to steer (in addition to weight-shift), and flare (during landing).

Weight Shift: In addition to manipulating the brakes, a paraglider pilot must also lean in order to steer properly. Such 'weight-shifting' can also be used for more limited steering when brake use is unavailable, such as when under 'big ears' (see below). More advanced control techniques may also involve weight-shifting.

Speed Bar: A kind of foot control called the 'speed bar' (also 'accelerator') attaches to the paragliding harness and connects to the leading edge of the paraglider wing, usually through a system of at least two pulleys (see animation in margin). This control is used to increase speed, and does so by decreasing the wing's angle of attack. This control is necessary because the brakes can only slow the wing from what is called 'trim speed' (no brakes applied). The accelerator is needed to go faster than this.

More advanced means of control can be obtained by manipulating the paraglider's risers or lines directly:

- Most commonly, the lines connecting to the outermost points of the wing's leading edge can be used to induce the wingtips to fold under. The technique, known as 'big ears', is used to increase rate of descent (see picture and therefore description below).
- The risers connecting to the rear of the wing can also be manipulated for steering if the brakes have been severed or are otherwise unavailable.
- In a 'B-line stall'

Fast Descents

Problems with "getting down" can occur when the lift situation is very good or when the weather changes unexpectedly. There are three possibilities of rapidly reducing altitude in such situations, each of which has benefits and issues to be aware of:

- Big ears induces descent rates of 2m/s or so. It is the most controllable of the techniques, and the easiest for beginners to learn.
- A B-line stall induces descent rates of 5m/s or so. It increases loading on parts of the wing (the pilot's weight is mostly on the B-lines, instead of spread across all the lines). There is not a risk of the pilot becoming disoriented as a result of using this technique.
- A spiral dive offers the fastest rate of descent, at 10-15m/sec. It places greater loads on the wing than other techniques do, and requires the highest level of skill from the pilot to execute safely.

Big Ears

By pulling on the outer A-lines the wing tips of the glider can be folded in. This method drastically deteriorates the glide angle with only a small decrease in forward speed. The effectiveness of this technique can be increased by using the speed system at the same time.

To reinflate on a low performance glider (e.g. DHV1 rated) it is simply necessary to release the lines. On higher performance gliders (e.g. DHV1/2 and above) it may be necessary to help the reinflation with brief, deep pumps of the brakes.

Whilst big ears are in use, the loading on the remaining flying surface of the glider is increased and it is therefore more stable and less prone to collapse. However there is an increased risk of stalling because 'pulling the ears' increases the angle of attack and reduces the speed of the wing. So while 'ears' and speed bar is a good combination, 'ears' and brake is not - it is best not to use the brakes when the ears are 'in'.

B-Line stall

In a 'B-line stall', the second set of risers from the leading-edge/front (the B-lines) are pulled down independently of the other risers; with the specific lines used to initiate the condition being responsible for its name. This puts a crease in the upper surface of the wing, thereby destroying the laminar flow of air over the aerofoil. This dramatically reduces the lift produced by the canopy and thus induces a higher rate of descent.

The B-line stall should be initiated with the wing in normal flight (no speed bar; not accelerated). Grasp the B-lines on both sides above the line links and pull them down. There is no need to release the brake toggles while B-stalling. DHV 1/2 wings are very resistant to creasing; the pilot may have to pull on the B-lines with sufficient force to almost lift themselves out of the seat to get the wing to crease. Once the crease is in, it requires less effort to keep it in that it does to initiate it.

The sensation for the pilot when the B-line stall is induced is that the breeze is upwards rather than in your face. Pulling the B-lines even further down will not enhance the sink rate, but can lead to a more unstable flight position.

To recover from the B-line stall, release the B-risers so that the aerofoil shape of the wing is resumed. This will normally be sufficient to resume normal flight, but if the canopy remains in a stall push forward gently on the A-risers to lower the leading edge of the wing and reattach the laminar airflow to the upper surface of the wing.

Spiral Dive

The spiral dive is the most rapid form of controlled fast descent. With a little bit of practice you will achieve a sink rate of 15 m/s and more.

However, spiral dives put strong G-forces on the wing and glider and must be done carefully and skilfully. The G-forces involved can induce blackouts, and the rotation can produce disorientation. Spiral dives, as with all paragliding techniques, are best learned under expert supervision. Paragliding 'SIV' courses offer a chance to practice spiral dives over water with a rescue boat standing by.

The spiral dive is initiated by pulling the brake on one side and holding it down. Constant pulling on one brake narrows the radius of the turn and forms a spiral rotation in which high sink rates can be reached. As soon as the glider is in a spiral dive (clear increase of sink rate and turn bank), the outside wing should always be stabilised with the outside brake and the desired sink rate should be controlled with great delicacy.

Flying

Launching

As with all aircraft, launching and landing are done into wind (though in mountain flying, it is possible to launch in nil wind and glide out to the first thermal).

Forward Launch

In low winds, the wing is inflated with a 'forward launch', where the pilot runs forward so that the air pressure generated by the forward movement inflates the wing.

Reverse Launch

In higher winds, particularly ridge soaring, a 'reverse launch' is used, with the pilot facing the wing to bring it up into a flying position, then turning under the wing to complete the launch.

Reverse launches have a number of advantages over a forward launch. It is more straight forward to inspect the wing and check the lines are free as it leaves the ground. In the presence of wind, the pilot can be tugged toward the wing and facing the wing makes it easier to resist this force, and safer in case the pilot slips (as opposed to being dragged backwards). These launches are normally attempted with a reasonable wind speed making the ground speed required to pressurise the wing much lower - the pilot is initially launching while walking forwards as opposed to running backward.

Towed Launch

In flatter countryside pilots can also be launched with a tow. Once at full height, the pilot pulls a release cord and the towline falls away. This requires separate training, as flying on a winch has quite different characteristics from free flying. There are two major ways to tow: Pay-in and pay-out towing. Pay-in towing involves a stationary winch that pays in the towline and thereby pulls the pilot in the air. The distance between winch and pilot at the start is around 500 meters or more. Pay-out towing involves a moving object, like a car or a boat, that pays out line slower than the speed of the object thereby pulling the pilot up in the air. In both cases it is very important to have a gauge indicating daN to avoid pulling the pilot out of the air. There is one other form of towing; 'static' towing. This involves a moving object, like a car or a boat, attached to a paraglider or hanglider with a fixed length line. This is very dangerous because now the forces on the line have to be controlled by the moving object itself, which is almost impossible to do. With static line towing a lockout is bound to happen sooner or later. Static line towing is forbidden in most countries and if not, should be avoided at all cost.

Landing

Landing involves lining up for an approach into wind, and just before touching down, 'flaring' the wing to minimise horizontal speed. In light winds, some minor running is common. In moderate to medium headwinds, the landings can be without forward speed.

Slope Soaring

The slope can be a Dune or Ridge. In slope soaring, pilots fly along the length of a slope feature in the landscape, relying on the lift provided by the air which is forced up as it passes over the slope. Slope soaring is highly dependent on a steady wind within a defined range (the suitable range depends on the performance of the wing and the skill of the pilot). Too little wind, and insufficient lift is available to stay airborne (pilots end up 'scratching' along the slope). With more wind, gliders can fly well above and forward of the slope, but too much wind, and there is a risk of being 'blown back' over the slope.

Thermal Flying

When the sun warms the ground, it will warm some features more than others (such as rock-faces or large buildings), and these set off thermals which rise through the air. Sometimes these may be a simple rising column of air; more often, they are blown sideways in the wind, and will break off from the source, with a new thermal forming later.

Once a pilot finds a thermal, he or she begins to fly in a circle, trying to center the circle on the strongest part of the thermal (the "core"), where the air is rising the fastest. Most pilots use a 'vario' (vario-altimeter), which indicates climb rate with beeps and/or a visual display, to help 'core-in' on a thermal.

Coring: The technique to "core" a thermal is simple: turn tighter as lift decreases, and turn less as lift increases. This ensures you are always flying around the core.

Often there is strong sink surrounding thermals, and there is often also strong turbulence resulting in wing collapses as a pilot tries to enter a strong thermal. Once inside a thermal, shear forces reduce somewhat and the lift tends to become smoother.

Good thermal flying is a skill which takes time to learn, but a good pilot can often "core" a thermal all the way to cloud base.

Cross-country Flying

Once the skills of using thermals to gain altitude have been mastered, pilots can glide from one thermal to the next to go 'cross-country' ('XC'). Having gained altitude in a thermal, a pilot glides down to the next available thermal. Potential thermals can be identified by land features which typically generate thermals, or by cumulus clouds which mark the top of a rising column of warm, humid air as it reaches the dew point and condenses to form a cloud. In many flying areas, cross-country pilots also need an intimate familiarity with air law, flying regulations, aviation maps indicating restricted airspace, etc.

In-flight Wing Deflation

Since the shape of the wing (airfoil) is formed by the moving air entering and inflating the wing, in turbulent air, part or all of the wing (airfoil) can deflate (collapse). Piloting techniques referred to as "active flying" will greatly reducc the frequency and severity of deflations or collapses. On modern recreational wings, such deflations will normally recover without pilot intervention. In the event of a severe deflation, correct pilot input will speed recovery from a deflation, but incorrect pilot input may slow the return of the glider to normal flight, so pilot training and practice in correct response to deflations is necessary. For the rare occasions when it is not possible to recover from a deflation (or from other threatening situations such as a spin), most pilots carry a reserve (rescue, emergency) parachute. Most pilots never have cause to 'throw' their reserve. Should a wing deflation occur at low altitude, i.e. shortly after takeoff or just before landing, the wing (paraglider) may not recover its correct structure rapidly enough to prevent an accident, with the pilot often not having enough altitude remaining to successfully deploy a reserve parachute (with the minimum altitude for this being approximately 200 ft, but typical deployment to stabilization periods using up 400 - 600 ft of altitude). Different packing methods of the reserve parachute affect its deploying time. It is also important to note that, should the wing collapse have been due to turbulence, this 'bad air' can cause the reserve parachute to take significantly longer to inflate and stabilise. In this example, it may be of greater benefit to the paraglider to purposefully lose altitude to 'clear' this turbulent air before deploying their reserve; should they have spare altitude to use on this process. Low altitude wing failure can result in serious injury or death due to the subsequent velocity of a ground impact where, ironically, a higher altitude failure may allow more time to regain some degree of control in the descent rate and, critically, deploy the reserve if needed. In-flight wing deflation and other hazards are minimized by flying a suitable glider and choosing appropriate weather conditions and locations for the pilot's skill and experience level.

Sports/competitive Flying

Some pilots like to stretch themselves beyond recreational flying. For such pilots, there are multiple disciplines available:

- Cross-country leagues - annual leagues of the greatest distance 'XC' flying
- "Comps" - competitive flying based on completing a number of tasks such as flying around set waypoints
- Accuracy - spot landing competitions where pilots land on targets with a 3 cm centre spot out to a full 10 meter circle.
- "Acro" - aero-acrobatic manoeuvres and stunt flying; heart stopping tricks such as helicopters, wing-overs, synchro spirals, infinity tumbles, and so on.
- National/international records - despite continually improving gliders, these become ever more difficult to achieve; aside from longest distance and highest altitude, examples include distance to declared goal, distance over triangular course, speed over 100 km triangular course, etc.

Competitive flying is done on high performance wings which demand far more skill to fly than their recreational counterparts, but which are far more responsive and offer greater feedback to the pilot, as well as flying faster with better glide ratios.

The current world champion is Andy Aebi of Switzerland; he won the title in February 2009 at Valle de Bravo in Mexico. His predecessor was Bruce Goldsmith.

There is great potential for injury for the unlucky, the reckless or ill-prepared. Safety is directly influenced by the pilot's mental attitude, experience, skill, reaction time, active nature of the air and whether or not the paraglider is flying at an altitude where the emergency reserve parachute might possibly have time to open in the event of an unrecoverable collapse or spiral dive. Incidents of any nature that happen in an altitude that does not allow to recover or deploy the reserve parachute (as while start and landing) are the most likely situtations to cause severe or fatal injuries.

Given that equipment failure of properly certified paragliding equipment can be considered a non-issue, it is accurate to say that paragliding can be a very safe sport. The individual pilot is the ultimate indicator of his or her personal safety level.

In general:

- The safe pilot will not fly at sites that pose an unreasonable challenge to his/her flying skills.
- The safe pilot will not be influenced by the possibly negative examples set by others.
- The safe pilot will only fly on days in which the weather is conducive to safe flight. Turbulence in all its forms is enemy #1 for a flying paraglider wing. Because paragliders have no solid support, their shape (and ability to fly) can be ruined by an errant down draft or the like. Therefore, turbulence or conditions conducive to turbulence generation is a primary factor in determining whether the weather is safe.

  The following weather is to be avoided:

- Excessive wind speed or gustiness. 15 mph (24 km/h) wind is fairly windy for a paraglider, and most pilots won't take off in much more wind than that. High winds will also increase the effect of mechanical turbulence. Gusty conditions will make take-offs and landings more dangerous and will make collapses more likely while in flight. The limit of 15 mph is fairly arbitrary, and also depends on local parameters. At some sites people fly safely at 20 mph winds, at other sites 10 mph may be too much.

- A wind direction that will not allow a take-off (or landing) into the wind, or at least generally so. Tail-wind take-offs are to be avoided at all cost. Assurance that an [apparent] headwind is not actually a 'rotor' is also critical (rotors comprise a form of mechanical turbulence).
- Excessively high atmospheric instability, indicated in part by overdeveloped cumulus clouds, or in worse situations by cumulo-nimbus cloud formation. Such conditions will contribute to turbulence. If cumulo-nimbus (thunderstorm) clouds are anywhere in sight, the effect of severe atmospheric instability may exist where you are.
- Rain or snow. Because a paraglider wing is made from fabric, it has the ability to absorb moisture. Moreover, the weight (or lack thereof) of a paraglider wing is critical to its performance. Flying into heavy rain or snow will weigh the wing down and may terminate a flight quickly. A wet wing is also less controllable, less stable and will exhibit less tendency to recover into normal flight.

General safety precautions include pre-flight checks, helmets, harnesses with back protection (foam or air-bag), reserve parachutes, and careful pre-launch observation of other pilots in the air to evaluate conditions.

For pilots who want to stretch themselves into more challenging conditions, advanced 'SIV' (simulation d'incidents en vol, or simulation of flying incidents) courses are available to teach pilots how to cope with hazardous situations which can arise in flight. Through instruction over radio (above a lake), pilots deliberately induce major collapses, stalls, spins, etc, in order to learn procedures for recovering from them. (As mentioned above, modern recreational wings will recover from minor collapses without intervention).

As always, fatalities and freak accidents can occur, but most properly-trained, responsible pilots risk only minor injuries, such as twisted ankles.

Learning to Fly

Most popular paragliding regions have a number of schools, generally registered with and/or organized by national associations. Certification systems vary widely between countries, though around 10 days instruction to basic certification is standard.

There are several key components to a paragliding pilot certification instruction program. Initial training for beginning pilots usually begins with some amount of ground school to discuss the basics, including elementary theories of flight as well as basic structure and operation of the paraglider.

Students then learn how to control the glider on the ground, practicing take-offs and controlling the wing 'overhead'. Low, gentle hills are next where students get their first short flights, flying at very low altitudes, to get used to the handling of the wing over varied terrain. Special winches can be used to tow the glider to low altitude in areas that have no hills readily available.

As their skills progress, students move on to steeper/ higher hills (or higher winch tows), making longer flights, and learning to turn the glider, control the glider's speed, then moving on to 360° turns, spot landings, 'big ears' (used to increase the rate of descent for the paraglider), and other more advanced techniques. Training instructions are often provided to the student via radio, particularly during the first flights.

A third key component to a complete paragliding instructional program provides substantial background in the key areas of meteorology, aviation law, and general flight area etiquette.

To give prospective pilots a chance to determine if they would like to proceed with a full pilot training program, most schools offer tandem flights, in which an experienced instructor pilots the paraglider with the prospective pilot as a passenger. Schools often offer pilot's families and friends the opportunity to fly tandem, and sometimes sell tandem pleasure flights at holiday resorts.

Most recognised courses lead to a national licence and an internationally recognised International Pilot Proficiency Information/Identification card. The IPPI specifies five stages of paragliding proficiency, from the entry level ParaPro 1 to the most advance stage 5.

World Records

FAI (Fédération Aéronautique Internationale) world records:

- Straight distance - 502.9 km: Nevil Hulett (South Africa); Copperton - Lesotho, South Africa; 14 December 2008.
- Previous Straight distance - 461.6 km: Frank Brown, Marcelo Prieto, Rafael Monteiro Saladini (Brazil); Quixada - Duque, Brazil; 14 November 2007.
- Straight distance - 411.3 km: Nevil Hulett (South Africa); Copperton - Lesotho, South Africa; 14 December 2008.
- Previous Straight distance to declared goal - 368.9 km: Aljaž Vali?, Urban Vali? (Slovenia); Vosburg - Jamestown (South Africa); 7 December 2006
- Gain of height - 4526 m: Robbie Whittall (UK); Brandvlei (South Africa); 6 January 1993

Other records (distance/speed for out-and-return and triangular course) can be seen on the FAI site

Recently a flight of over 500 km was made by Nevil Hulett in excellent conditions in South Africa; Flight record

Chapter-6

LOOKING FOR ECO FAUNA

For the wildlife enthusiast India is the place that simply offers large variety of animal and bird-life. India holds for about 400 species of mammals and 1200 species of birds. Wildlife Safari in India is probably the best way to explore the rich flora and fauna and get close to the mother nature. To get the fascinating experience of the rich wildlife go through the different National Parks and Wildlife sanctuaries in India. In totality India is the home to 80 National Parks and 440 Wildlife Sanctuaries. If you are going for the wildlife tour in India, you must live there for three to four days, to meet the wilds in their natural habitat. Spend time listening to the melodious and chirping sounds of the birds, spot the tigers in the wild, sleep in the open tents under the dark starry night. Tiger is the National animals and Peacock is the National Bird of India. These parks are vital for the protection and conservation of the endangered species such as Royal Bengal Tigers, Indian Elephants, Indian Rhinos, Siberian Crane, leopards and lions.

Sambar Deer		Classification
Kingdom	:	Animalia
Phylum	:	Chordata
Class	:	Mammalia
Order	:	Artiodactyla

Suborder	:	Ruminantia
Family	:	Cervidae
Subfamily	:	Cervinae
Genus	:	Cervus
Species	:	C. unicolor
Zoological name	:	Cervus unicolor
Found In	:	Kanha, Corbett, Ranthambore, Bandhavgarh, Gir, Dudhwa, Manas, Kaziranga National Park in India

Physical appearance : Sambar deed stands to a height of 135 -150 cm at the shoulder and can weigh up to 300 kg. Males have antlers measuring up to 1m. Its coat is dark brown in colour. It is characterized with large muzzle and broad ears. It has tick fur and orange spots on its body. Males are larger than the females. Its tail is 22- 35 cm long. Males have thick mane of hairs around the neck.

Presence in India : Sambar deer is found in almost every corner of India, But it is mainly found in the central India. They can easily be spotted at Kanha, Corbett, Ranthambore, Bandhavgarh, Gir, Dudhwa, Manas, Kaziranga and Sariska.

Habitat : Sambar Deer prefers marshy and wooded areas to live.

Diet : Sambar deer feeds on leaves, vegetation, herbs, fruit, bamboo buds and mushrooms.

Reproduction :The breeding period is mainly during the months of November and December. The gestation period rests for almost 6 months after which single offspring is born. The young ones are weaned at about 7 months of age.

Conservation status : Least concern

Lifespan : The life expectancy of Sambar Deer exceeds up to 18 -20 years of age.

Neelgai		Classification
Kingdom	:	Animalia
Phylum	:	Chordata
Class	:	Mammalia
Order	:	Artiodactyla
Family	:	Bovidae
Subfamily	:	Bovinae
Genus	:	Boselaphus
Species	:	B. tragocamelus
Zoological name	:	Boselaphus tragocamelus
Found In	:	SariskaTiger Reserve, Ranthambore National Park and Sultanpur Bird Sanctuary

Physical appearance : Neelgai is 6- 7 feet long and weigh around 120 -240 kg. They are 4- 5 feet tall. They have erectile mane on the nape and back and the hair pennant in the middle of the underside of the neck. They have white spot on their cheeks, lips and throat Along the underside is a thin white stripe, which "balloons" at the rear. They have long and slender head. Males have 8 -10 inch long horns. It has relatively small horns. Their tail is 40- 45 cm long.Male coat is gray blue and female coat is yellow brown in colour.

Presence in India : Neelgai are widely found in the jungles of Karnataka, Rajasthan, West Bengal, Assam and Haryana. They are also commonly seen in some of the National parks and wildlife Sanctuaries such as Sariska, Ranthambore, Panna and Sultanpur.

Habitat : Neelgai prefers to live in open plains, woodlands, dense jungles and grasslands.

Diet : Neelgai feeds on plants, seeds, branches, leaves, fruit, flowers, stems and buds.

Reproduction : Neelgai reach the level of sexual maturity in 18 months. They do not have any specific breeding season. The gestation period rests for 275 days. Usually twins are born at a time. Young ones weigh around 30 -35 pounds.

Conservation status : Declared by the IUCN as being at low risk of extinction.

Lifespan : Neelgai lives up to 20- 30 years of age.

Royal Bengal Tiger		**Classification**
Kingdom	:	Animalia
Phylum	:	Chordata
Class	:	Mammalia
Order	:	Carnivora
Family	:	Felidae
Genus	:	Panthera
Subspecies	:	P. t. tigris
Species	:	P.tigris
Zoological name	:	Panthera tigris tigris
Found In	:	Corbett, Manas, Bandipur, Sariska, Kanha, Ranthambore and Sundarbans National Park.

Physical appearance : Royal Bengal Tigers are 6 - 9 feet long and weigh around 400- 600 pounds. They have large head, big ears and thick whickers. Its fur are reddish gold in colour. They have stripes all over their body. Males are usually larger than the females. Their tail is 3 feet long. They have large padded paws with retractable claws. They have white spot on the back of their ears, which looks like eyes. Bengal Tigers have great vision and strong sense of smell.

Presence in India : Royal Bengal Tigers are easily found in the jungles of West Bengal, Madhya Pradesh, Assam, Rajasthan, Orissa, Uttar Pradesh and Tamil Nadu. They are also spotted in some of the major National Parks and Wildlife Sanctuaries of India such as Corbett, Manas, Bandipur, Sariska, Kanha, Ranthambore and Sundarbans National Park.

Habitat : Royal Bengal Tigers prefers dense forests and lush grasslands.

Diet : Bengal Tigers are carnivorous. They feed on large variety of mammals such as deer, antelope, pigs, buffaloes, humans, wild boars, gaurs, hares, monkeys, wild ox, langur, peacocks, wolves, crocodiles, dholes and many more.

Reproduction :Bengal Tiger reach the level of sexual maturity in 3- 4 years of age. They usually mate during the spring season. Gestation period rests for 95 -112days after which the tigress give birth to two to four cubs.

Conservation status : Highly endangered

Lifespan : Lifespan of the Royal Bengal Tigers exceeds up to the 15 years of age.

Physical appearance : The average height of the Indian Elephant is estimated to be about 7 to 12 feet and weighs anything between 3,600 kg to 5000 kg. The length of their head and body is around 550 to 640 cm and shoulder height is 250 to300 cm. They have thick and dry skin. The colour of their skin varies from grey to brown. They have smaller ears which are straight at the bottom, an arched back and a single finger like proturbance that is located at the tip of the trunk. Their brain weigh around 5kg.They have unique modified incisor teeth known as tusks. Their heart beat 28 times a minute. They are considered as the endangered species.

Presence in India : The Indian Elephants are found in the wild in the dense forested areas of India including tropical forests of South India, North East India and the Sub Himalayan Region. Manas, Corbett, Dalma and Palamu, Bandipur and Nagarhole, Periyar and Madumalai are the best places to watch the Asian Elephants in its natural habitat.

Habitat : Indian Elephants live in different habitat in open grassland, marshes and savannas. They can also be found in jungles, water sources and mountainous regions.

Diet : The Indian Elephants mostly feeds on a wide variety of grasses. They are also dependent upon cultivated crops, bark, root, twigs, fruits and leaves. They are one among the herbivorous animals. An adult elephant can consume up to 300 pounds of food in a single day.

Reproduction :There is no specific mating season for the Indian Elephants. Both males ans females become sexually mature at about 14 years of age. The gestation period is usually 20- 22 months and the females have the capability of giving birth to a calf in every four to five years. At birth elephants can be one meter tall and weigh around ninety kilograms. They can stand soon after the birth. Female elephants supervise their young ones for several years after weaning.

Conservation status : The population of the Indian Elephants lies somewhere between 38,000 and 51,000. They have been continuously haunted by the people for the food, for ivory and for the domestic stock. They have suffered the great habitat loss due to the deforestation and agriculture.

Lifespan : Lifespan of the Indian Elephants is about 70 years.

Indian Camel is 6 feet long and weighs around 700 kg. It is 7 feet high from its hump. It tail is 50 cm long. It is characterized by long curved neck, large mouth and high hump. They are usually brown or black in colour. Camel's nasal passages are properly covered with the large muscular nostrils. Camels have thin, long and powerful legs. They have large eyes with long eyelashes and bushy eyebrows.but small ears. Indian camels have broad, flat and leathery pads with two toes on each foot with leathery patches on their knees.

Species : Camelus bactrianus, Camelus dromodariuo, Camelus gigas, Camelus hesternus, Camelus sivalensis

Presence in India : India Camel is mostly found in the North Western part of India.They are also spotted in the Kaziranga and Desert National Park.

Habitat : Camels mostly prefer dry places.

Diet : Camels are herbivorous. They feed on grass, grains, wheat, oats, dried leaves, and seeds . As their humps contain fat, they can go without food for 3-4 days.

Reproduction : Camels reach the level of sexual maturity at 4-5 years of age. The gestation period lasts for 13 months after which the a single calf is born. The calves start walking within two hours of birth.

Conservation status : IUCN Red List of Threatened species.

Lifespan : Camel lives up to the 40 years of age.

Indian subcontinent has a rich and varied biodiversity to boast of. Infact, the country is home to some of the most rare as well as magnificent wild animals. Most of the wild animals of India are being protected from poaching as well as habitat loss through the numerous national parks and wildlife sanctuaries. Indian culture preaches respect for each and every form of life, including wildlife. Still, greedy individuals as well as the ever-increasing population are putting pressure on the peaceful existence of Indian wild animals. In this section, we have provided information on the following wild animals living in India:

Indian Asiatic Lion

Asiatic Lions once used to roam around the area, stretching from northern Greece, across Southwest Asia, to central India. However, today the natural habitat of the majestic animal has been reduced to the Gir forests of India only, making the Asiatic Lion almost synonymous with the Indian Lion.

Bengal Tiger

Bengal tiger is a subspecies of tiger, which is found in the Bengal region of the Indian subcontinent. One of the most common tiger subspecies, it is also found in a number of other Asian countries, like Bangladesh, Nepal, Bhutan, Myanmar, Tibet, etc.

Indian Black Bear

Indian black bear is also known by the names of Asiatic Black Bear (Ursus thibetanus), Tibetan black bear, Himalayan black bear and Moon bear. They grow to a length of approximately 4 to 6 feet, right from the nose to the tail.

Indian Black Buck

Indian black buck is also known by a number of other names like Kala Hiran, Sasin, Iralai Maan and Krishna Jinka. The scientific name of the black buck antelope is Antilope cervicapra and it natural habitat is the Indian subcontinent.

Indian Camel

The camels found in India are the single-humped camels, also known as the Dromedary camels. Long-curved neck, deep-narrow chest and a single hump characterize the Indian camel.

Indian Clouded Leopard

Clouded leopards belong to the Neofelis genus and have the scientific name of Neofelis nebulosa. The average lifespan of a clouded leopard is 11 years in the wild. However, in cases of captivity, it may go upto 17 years.

Indian Deer

The name 'Deer' is given to the ruminant mammals belonging to the family Cervidae. They are one of the most beautiful creatures on this earth and extend to approximately 34 species.

Indian Elephant

Indian elephant, known with the scientific name of 'Elephas maximus indicus', is a subspecies of the Asian Elephant. It is mainly found in the Indian subcontinent, that to in the scrub forested areas.

Indian Langur

Indian langurs are lanky, long-tailed monkeys, having bushy eyebrows and a chin tuft. They have a black face and their body color ranges from gray to dark brown to golden.

Indian Leopard

Indian leopard is one of the 8-9 valid leopard subspecies found throughout the world. Known by the scientific name of Panthera pardus, it is the fourth largest of the four 'big cats' of the Panthera genus.

Indian Macaque

Macaques are considered to be the second most-widespread species in the world, after humans. Their range stretches on from northern Africa to Japan. Macaques comprise of 22 species in toto, out of which seven can be found in India also.

Indian Red Panda

Red panda is a beautiful animal, found in only some other countries of the world, including the Indian subcontinent. Scientifically known as Ailurus fulgens, it is slightly bigger than the domestic cat and founds a mention in the list of endangered species.

Indian Rhinoceros

Indian Rhinoceros holds the distinction of being the fourth largest animal, after the three elephant species. Known by the scientific name of Rhinoceros unicornis, the animal is found in only two places in the world, Assam (India) and Nepal.

Indian Snow Leopard

Snow leopard is a native animal of mountain ranges of central and southern Asia, including India. It is also known as Ounce and has a scientific name of "Panthera uncia". Snow leopards can live for a maximum of 18 years in then wild.

Indian Striped Hyena

Striped hyena belongs to the Hyaenidae family and is scientifically known as Hyaena hyaena. Strongly related to the Brown hyena, it is basically a solitary creature. The average lifespan of striped hyenas hovers somewhere around 10 to 12 years in the wild.

Indian Wild Ass

Indian wild ass, also known as khur, is one of the subspecies of wild ass belonging to southern Asia. Its scientific name is Equus hemionus khur. Wild ass of India has an average age of 20-25 years.

Indian Wild Boar

Wild boar is considered to be the wild antecedent of the domestic pig of the Indian subcontinent. It belongs to the Suidae biological family, which also includes the Warthog and Bushpig of Africa, the Pygmy Hog of northern India and the Babirusa of Indonesia.

The Common Muntjac, also called Indian Muntjac (Muntiacus muntjak) is the most numerous muntjac deer species. It has soft, short, brownish or greyish hair, sometimes with creamy markings. This species is omnivorous, feeding on fruits, shoots, seeds, birds' eggs as well as small animals and even carrion. It gives calls similar to barking, usually on sensing a predator (hence the common name for all muntjacs of barking deer).

The male Indian Muntjac has small antlers which attain 15 cm in length and have only 1 branch. They grow annually from a bony stalk on the head. Males are extremely territorial and can be fierce for their size. They will fight each other for territory using their antlers or their (more dangerous) tusk-like upper canine teeth, and can defend themselves against predators such as dogs.

The Indian Muntjac (Muntiacus muntjak) is also commonly called the "barking deer" due to the bark-like sound that it makes as an alarm when danger is present. It is also called "Karkar". Sometimes these deer will bark for an hour or more. This species is one of eleven different species of Muntjacs spread across Asia. The Indian Muntjacs specifically are widespread throughout Southern Asia, but are one of the least known Asian animals. Paleontological evidence proves that Indian Muntjacs have been around since the late Pleistocene epoch at least 12,000 years ago. Since then, they have played a major role in Southern Asia for sport hunting as well as being hunted for its meat and skin. Often, these animals are hunted around the outskirts of agricultural areas because they can be considered a nuisance damaging crops and ripping bark off of trees. However, this animal is still in an abundance in Southern Asia numbering anywhere from 140,000-150,000 in India alone as of 2004.

Description

The Indian Muntjac has a short but very soft, thick, dense coat, especially those living in cooler regions. Coloration of the coat changes from dark brown to yellowish and grayish brown depending on the season. The Muntjacs' coat is golden tan on the dorsal side and white on the ventral side of the body, the limbs are dark brown to reddish brown, and the face is dark brown. However, the ears have very little hair which barely covers them. Male muntjacs have antlers that are very short, about 1-2 inches, usually consisting of only two or three points at the most and protrude from long body hair covered pedicels on the forehead. Females have tufts of fur and small bony knobs where the antlers are located in males. Males also have slightly elongated upper canines about an inch long that curve slightly outward from the lips and have the capability to inflict serious injury upon other animals or to other members of the population while exhibiting aggression. Males are generally larger than females. The body length of Muntjacs varies from 35-53 in.Their height ranges from 15-26 in.

Habitat

The Indian Muntjac is among the most widespread but least known of all the animals in South Asia. This species is distributed throughout South Asia, but more densely located in Southeastern Asia. Some specific countries the Indian Muntjac is found in are Northeastern India, bangladesh, Sri Lanka, Nepal, Southern China, Vietnam, the Malay peninsula, Riau Archipelago, Sumatra, Bangka, Belitung Islands, Java, Bali, and Borneo. The Muntjac is usually found in plentiful forests and places with dense vegetation such as grasslands, savannas, tropical deciduous forests, and tropical scrub forests. They are also very populated in the hilly country on the slopes of the Himalayas. They are found at both sea level and medium height altitudes up to 9,800 ft. They never wander far from water. Also, males usually have their own territory which may overlap the territories of a few females but not of another male.Somtimes in cambodia too.

Diet

The Indian Muntjacs are classified as omnivores. They are considered both browsers and grazers with a diet consisting of grasses, ivy, prickly bushes, low growing leaves, bark, twigs, herbs, fruit, sprouts, seeds, tender shoots, bird eggs and small warm-blooded animals. Indian Muntjacs are typically found feeding at the edge of the forest or in abandoned clearings.

Their large canines help in the processes of retrieving and ingesting food.

Reproduction

The Indian Muntjacs are polygamous animals. Females sexually mature during their first to second year of life. These females are polyestrous, with each cycle lasting about 14 to 21 days and an estrus lasting for 2 days. The gestation period is six to seven months and they usually bear one offspring at a time but sometimes produce twins. Females usually give birth in dense growth so that they are hidden from the rest of the herd and predators. The young leaves its mother after about six months to establish its own territory. Males often fight between one another for possession of a harem of females. Indian Muntjacs are distinguished from other ungulates in showing no evidence of a specific breeding season within the species.

Behavior

Indian Muntjacs are regarded as extremely solitary animals, rarely observed with other muntjacs, except for a mother and her young and during the rutting season. Males acquire territories that they mark with scent markers by rubbing their frontal preorbital gland (located on their head) on the ground and on trees, scraping their hooves against the ground, and scraping the bark of trees with their lower incisors. These scent markers allow other Muntjacs to know whether a territory is occupied or not. Males will often fight with each other over these territories, sufficient vegetation, and for primary preference over females when mating using their short antlers and an even more dangerous weapon, their canines. If a male is not strong enough to acquire his own territory he will most likely become prey to a leopard or some other predator. During the time of the rut, territorial lines are temporarily disregarded and overlap while males roam constantly in search of a receptive female.

These deer are incredibly alert creatures. When put into a stressful situation or if a predator is sensed, Muntjacs will begin making a bark-like sound. Barking was originally thought of as a means of communication between the deer during mating season as well as an alert. However, in more recent studies it has been identified as a mechanism used solely in alarming situations meant to cause a predator to realize that it has been detected and move elsewhere or to reveal itself. The barking mechanism is used more frequently when visibility is reduced and can last for over an hour regarding one incident.

Muntjacs exhibit both diurnality and nocturnality.

Evolution and Scientific Classification

The appearance and evolution of ungulates came about at the beginning of the Tertiary epoch. These ungulates were members of the order Condylarthra which eventually gave rise to the Eparctocyon line. The Eparctocyon line includes the order Artiodactyla to which the present ungulate, Muntiacus muntjak, belongs. Ancestors of the Muntjac evolved or possessed an efficient compact ankle, small side toes, complicated premolars, and an almost completely covered mastoid bone. Cervids arose later from Palaeomerycid ancestry during the Oligocene epoch.

Members of the family Cervidae are described as deer where males possess bony antlers that molt annually (except in the Chinese water deer) and where the females lack antlers (except in reindeer). They range in North & South America, Europe, Asia, and northern Africa.

Kingdom: Animalia, Phylum: Chordata, Class: Mammalia, Order: Artiodactyla, Suborder: Ruminantia, Family: Cervidae, Subfamily: Muntiacinae, Genus: Muntiacus, Species: muntjak

There are 3 other subfamilies of Cervidae: Cervinae (deer & fallow deer), Hydropotinae (Chinese water deer), and Capriolinae (moose & reindeer).

There are 6 species of Muntjacs: M. atherodes (Borneo), M. reevesi (southern China, Taiwan), M. feae (south-central China, Laos, Burma, Thailand), M. gongshanensis (northwestern Yunnan, Tibet), M. crinifrons (southeastern China), and M. muntjak.

There are 15 subspecies of the Muntjac: M. m. annamensis, M. m. aureus, M. m. bancanus, M. m. curvostylis, M. m. grandicornis, M. m. malabaricus, M. m. montanus, M. m. muntjak, M. m. nainggolani, M. m. nigripes, M. m. peninsulae, M. m. pleicharicus, M. m. robinsoni, M. m. rubidus, M. m. vaginalis.

BIBLIOGRAPHY

- Honey, Martha (2008). Ecotourism and Sustainable Development: Who Owns Paradise? (Second ed.). Washington, DC: Island Press. pp. 33. ISBN 1597261254 ISBN 978-1597261258.

- Randall, A. (1987). Resource economics, Second Edition. New York, USA: John Wiley and Sons.

- also to do with social sustainability Honey, Martha (2008). Ecotourism and Sustainable Development: Who Owns Paradise? (Second ed.). Washington, DC: Island Press. pp. 29-31. ISBN 1597261254 ISBN 978-1597261258.

- Dasgupta, P. 2007. The idea of sustainable development,Sustainability Science, 2(1):5-11

- Heal, G., 2009. Climate Economics: A Meta-Review and Some Suggestions for Future Research, Review of Environmental Economics and Policy, 3(1):4-21

- Ayong Le Kama, 2001 A.D. Ayong Le Kama, Sustainable growth renewable resources, and pollution, Journal of Economic Dynamics and Control, 25:1911-1918

- Endress,L., J. Roumasset, and T. Zhou. 2005. Sustainable Growth with Environmental Spillovers,"Journal of Economic Behavior and Organization," 58(4):527-547,

- Arrow KJ, P. Dasgupta, L. Goulder, G Daily, PR Ehrlich, GM Heal, S Levin, K-G Maler, S Schneider, DA Starrett, B Walker.

2004. Are we consuming too much? Journal of Economic Perspectives, 18(3):147-172

- Asheim, G. 1999. Economic analysis of sustainability. In: W.M. Lafferty and O. Langhalle, Editors, Towards Sustainable Development, St. Martins Press, New York, p. 159
- Pezzey, J. 1989. Economic Analysis of Sustainable Growth and Sustainable Development, Environmental department Working Paper No. 15, World Bank.
- Barbier, E. 2007 Natural Resources and Economic Development, Cambridge University Press
- Jungmin Lee,(2004)Extreme Sports Evaluation: Evidence from Judging Figure Skating,Econometric Society
- Tomlinson, Joe (2004). Extreme Sports: In Search of the Ultimate Thrill. Hove: Firefly Books Ltd. ISBN 1-55297-992-X.
- "Ernest Hemingway FAQ part 5".
- "Extreme Sports - Encarta". Microsoft Encarta Online Encyclopedia. 2008. Archived from the original on 2009-10-31.
- "'Generation Y' Drives Increasingly Popular...". AmericanSportsData.com. August 1, 2002.
- Brymer, Eric and Gray, Tonia, Extreme Sports: A Challenge to Phenomenology. University of Wollongong, Australia, 2004
- Brymer, Eric, Extreme Dude: A Phenomenological Perspective on the Extreme sports experience . University of Wollongong, Australia, 2005
- Eadington, W.R., and V.L. Smith (1992). The emergence of alternative forms of tourism, in Tourism Alternatives: Potentials and Problems in the Development of Tourism. Pennsylvania, USA: University of Pennsylvania Press.
- Crinion, D. (1998). South Australian tourism strategy and the role of ecotourism. Adelaide, Australia: Down to Earth planning for an out-of-the-ordinary industry, presented at the South Australian Ecotourism Forum.

- Bar kin, D. (2002). Eco tourism for sustainable regional development. Current Issues in Tourism. pp. 5(3-4):245-253.
- Botanical Survey of India. 1983. Flora and Vegetation of India - An Outline. Botanical Survey of India, Howrah. 24 pp.
- Valmik Thapar, Land of the Tiger: A Natural History of the Indian Subcontinent, 1997.
- Tritsch, M.E. 2001. Wildlife of India Harper Collins, London. 192 pages. ISBN 0-00-711062-6
- K. Praveen Karanth. (2006). Out-of-India Gondwanan origin of some tropical Asian biota
- Groombridge, B. (ed). 1993. The 1994 IUCN Red List of Threatened Animals. IUCN, Gland, Switzerland and Cambridge, UK. lvi + 286 pp.
- Krausman, PR & AJT Johnsingh (1990) Conservation and wildlife education in India. Wildl. Soc. Bull. 18:342-347
- Project Tiger Accessed Feb, 2007
- Project Elephant Accessed Feb, 2007

Vivek Menon (2003). A field guide to Indian mammals. Dorling Kindersley, Delhi. ISBN 0143029983.

INDEX